Living Life Straight With No Chaser, The 30 Day Challenge
SLAYING THE INNER GIANT

Ms. Sabriena Ford – Williams
Author, Spiritual Life Coach, Ordained Pastor

1

Sabriena Ford-Williams
Copyright @ Sabriena M. Ford- Sheppard
All Rights Reserved

DEDICATION AND ACKNOWLEDGEMENTS

This book is dedicated to my two seeds Ja'kya Romea and Je'rod Harvey Sheppard. Thanks for allowing me to be your mother even through the hard times we have had to endure. I wanted to thank you both for being who God has ordained you to be. Without you both my life wouldn't have any meaning. You are both AMZING and I thank God for you. Ja'kya I know you are my daughter but, you have taught me so much about faith. When you chose to move to Texas on faith to follow your dreams, it made me realize that you were much stronger than I had given you credit for. You faith is EXPLOSIVE and God is going to do fabulous things in your life. You're smart, talented, gifted and anointed to finish what God has started in your life. I am very proud of you and don't you ever forget that .As a little girl you always had this fight to finish what you started and look it is really paying off. You will graduate with your second degree, you will own your own personal fitness business, and you will have the things your heart desires.

My only son Je'rod I decree and declare that the enemy will NOT have you. As a little boy you always desired to play football. You would run plays even when you were asleep. You talked about playing in the collegiate level for the University of Florida. I still believe in your dream and you will fulfill all the promises predestined for your life. Although there have been bumps along the way, I speak LIFE over your LIFE and you SHALL rightfully fulfill the dreams God implanted on the inside of you. I will never stop dreaming with you, praying for you and supporting you. May God richly bless both of you and never forget Mama Dukes loves you and there is nothing nobody can do about it. I dedicate this poem to you titled **"LOVE ENDLESS"**.

My Love for you is endless

My love for you stretches beyond the broad horizon

My heart will forever beat to your boundless rhythm

And dance to your overwhelming success, why

Because you – Ja'kya and Je'rod are the absolute best

My love for you flourishes when I see Gods promises being fulfilled through you

I am graciously applauding at the awesome things he has prepared for you to do

My love for you is endless

Never let go of the rope

I love you

Key Verse: The Giant
1 Samuel 17:45-48

David said to the Philistine, "You come against me with sword and spear and javelin, but I come against you in the name of the Lord Almighty, the God of the armies of Israel, whom you have defied. 46 This day the Lord will deliver you into my hands, and I'll strike you down and cut off your head. This very day I will give the carcasses of the Philistine army to the birds and the wild animals, and the whole world will know that there is a God in Israel. 47 All those gathered here will know that it is not by sword or spear that the Lord saves; for the battle is the Lord's, and he will give all of you into our hands."

48 As the Philistine moved closer to attack him, David ran quickly toward the battle line to meet him. 49 Reaching into his bag and taking out a stone, he slung it and struck the Philistine on the forehead. The stone sank into his forehead, and he fell face down on the ground.

Message from the Author
SLAYING THE GIANT WITHIN

Living Your Life Straight with No Chaser the 30 day Challenge- Slaying Your inner Giant is all about facing the dark truths in your life. Sometimes facing the truths requires some serious and rigorous discipline on our part. I must say everyone is not up to that type of challenge. The word Challenge in itself poses a threat to some.

According to the Webster Dictionary (2009), A Challenge is anything, as a demanding task, that calls for special effort or dedication. A challenge can also be viewed as a calling into question, a demanding of proof, or explanation. Before reading this book, I am demanding you to call your giant better known as your challenge to come under submission. I am pleading with you to give your challenge some needed attention. For a moment I won't you to reflect on the story of David and Goliath. David had a great challenge set before him. He had encountered a Giant that seemed unattainable to defeat. I hope by being this book you will be able to face your giant head on.

We all face Challenges. Whether the challenge is spiritual, mental, physical, psychological or financial, we have something that we will face while here on earth. Facing a challenge in your life can be extremely traumatic. I don't know anyone who can say they embrace change or challenges with open arms. I believe the reason why no one wants to openly embrace change is because change doesn't feel good. Change requires hard work. Change say's, there is a problem. Change draws attention to those who want to stay hidden. However, Change is a necessity to move forward. How many of you are willing to move forward? To be honest with ourselves, many of us would rather avoid a challenge.

To avoid a personal challenge some people resort to living a mundane life and unfortunately will never fully enjoy the desires and elations that God has positioned for them to feast upon. Although Challenges can be terrifying, we have to learn to face the biggest giant before us and that giant most times is one's self. We have to get to a place where we will fully accept responsibility for decisions that we have made while on this life course or accept the circumstances we may have been handed by life. When we don't fully deal with the giant it allows the spirit of fear and denial to submerge. If we are not careful this spirit of fear and denial will begin to slay us.

Denial is one of the factors that keep us impinged in the web of the giant. Oscar Wilde, DEProfundis says, "To regret one's own experiences are to arrest one's own development. To deny one's own experiences is to put a lie into lips of one's own life. It is no less than a denial of the soul. .

For some of us, the challenge is facing our childhood hurt. For others the challenge is getting over low self-esteem. Some people might be dealing with those feelings of abandonment by a husband who left them. Others could be trying to overcome the giant of homosexuality, fear, hurt, pain, shame, confusion, drug abuse, poverty or even depression.

I know personally my challenge was not feeling good enough or pretty enough. Feeling unworthy to compete with people in the world around me. I struggled with the complex of low self-worth. I allowed this giant to make me feel NOT GOOD ENOUGH .The giant of NOT GOOD ENOUGH suffocated me for many years. It was not until I developed a relationship with Jesus Christ that I understood that he made me in his image and I was good enough. I was more than good enough, I was uniquely designed. I was created with a purpose. I was his daughter of Zion and I was adopted in a family of royalty. After this great revelation I no longer allowed the giant to deny me access into the Kingdom of God.

Living Your Life Straight with No Chaser is unquestionably a book that will allow you to rest and reflect upon the past, present and future. Take a voyage with me as we embark upon this 30 day Challenge of rediscovering the Truth. We will ascertain the truth that the enemy has tried to exasperate the minds of Gods children with for many years. This 30 day challenge will give you enlightening words of encouragement that will allow you the reader to self-examine yourself and discover the TRUTH within you. This challenge will allow you to inspect the challenges as they have firmly secured themselves in your life. Like Goliath, this book is your sling shot. Your weapon to slay this giant that has bullied you over the years. Let's look at the story of David and Goliath.

David's faith in God caused him to look at the giant from a different view point. Goliath was merely a mortal man. David looked at the battle from God's point of view. If we look at giant problems and impossible situations from God's perspective, we begin to see that God will fight for us and with us. When we put things in proper order, we can see more clearly and we can fight more effectively. When the giant criticized, insulted and threatened, David didn't stop or even waver. Everyone else cowered in fear, but David ran to the battle. He knew that action needed to be taken. David did the right thing by facing his giant and not running the opposite direction. The most important factor to David was what God said about the matter. God said he was victorious and could overcome this giant. What has God said to you about your giant? Get ready for battle as you gird up your loins to assassinate this giant in your life. This will be the start of your victory dance. Get prepared to shout Hallelujah, Get prepared to set your captives free, Get prepared to conquer that fear. Tell yourself: My giant is coming down in Jesus name and now rejoice. As you read this book each thought provoking question should move you further and further towards the truth that resides on the inside of you. There is an answer within you to help you learn the strategies needed to defeat the giant that has tried to conquer the conquest before you.

Table of Contents
SLAYING THE GIANT WITHIN

Romans 12:2

Do not be conformed to this world, but be transformed by the renewal of your mind, that by testing you may discern what is the will of God, what is good and acceptable and perfect.

LIVING LIFE STRAIGHT WITH NO CHASER

The 30 DAY CHALLENGE

SLAYING THE GIANT WITHIN

Day 1

Challenge: Mindset Change: Think Outside The Box.

In an effort to overtake the giant you have to have a renewed mindset. What if David had decided in his mind that he just couldn't even stand up against the giant Goliath? David had to look at the situation from God's perceptive. He had to have the mindset of God.

When you face your giant you have to meditate like Christ. You have to negate the way the world thinks and fully expose your mind to the things of God. Romans 12:2 tells us, And be not conformed to this world : but be ye transformed by the renewing of your mind, that ye may prove what is good, and acceptable , and the perfect , will of God. The world will tell you that the giant is bigger, better, stronger, more apt to win the battle , but if you reflect on the word as it comes from 2 Corinthians 10:4-5 , it clearly says for the weapons of your warfare are not carnal but mighty through God to the pulling down of strong holds. Casting down imaginations, and every high thing that exalteth itself against the knowledge of God, and bringing into captivity every thought to the obedience of Christ.

The word for today is "TRY THINKING OUTSIDE THE BOX". When our minds are cluttered with low self-worth, hurt and rejection we fail to dream. We fail to think on those things that produce life and happiness. We fail to extend our thoughts past gloom and doom. We are dreamers by nature. I come to challenge you to take the blinders off and try thinking outside the box. Proverbs 29:28 reminds us that we must have a vision. Where there is no vision, the people perish: but he that keepeth the law, happy is he. Go with me for a second. Take your mind off the giant (problem) and tap into your desires and aspirations.

Have you ever desired to travel to a tropical island- wouldn't Hawaii be a refreshing experience? You will eat different types of food, Have a different cultural experience, perhaps go parasailing and become one with the air. You will have an opportunity to explore a new experience.

Try THINKING OUTSIDE THE BOX. The reason you have not thought outside the box is because the giant has confined your mind to thinking you CAN'T do it. The giant has impregnated you with fear. The giant has implanted anxieties, and panic into your mind. It has paralyzed your mind from grasping the true wonders of life.

We have to learn to slay the giant and experience life at a higher level than the one we are accustomed to. We have to slay the giant and declare that we no longer have to be bound to the social norms of the world. We have to "TRY THINKING OUTSIDE OF THE BOX". We cannot allow the fears, insecurities, past failures, hurts, shame and pain to keep us inside the box of life.

It is time that we live life and lives it more abundantly. Let go of the BOXED OUT mentality, and get inside the ring of life and LIVE. Refuse to let the angry stare of the giant scare you out of life. Do the things that excite your inner man, go laugh and play as you did as a child. "TRY THINKING OUTSIDE OF THE BOX". LIVE, LAUGH, LOVE, SHARE, GO, PLAN, EXPAND, INCREASE, and MARCH FORWARD, there is so much more on the other side of the box that awaits you. Are you willing to "TRY THINKING OUTSIDE OF THE BOX"? Go ahead give it a try; there is no failure in trying. Slay the giant with this thought. For God hath not given us the spirit of fear; but of power, and of love, and of a sound mind. 2 Timothy 1:7. Whatever it is that you aspire to do in life. Keep these words tucked snuggly in the comforts of your new mind. Fear thou not ; for I am with thee: be not dismayed ; for I am thy God: I will strengthen thee; yea , I will help thee; yea , I will uphold thee with the right hand of my righteousness. Isaiah 41:10.

THINKING OUTSIDE THE BOX PRAYER and SLAYING THE INNER GIANT:

Father God I ask that this reader will no longer subject their mind to the things of this world but be renewed by the things of God. May every evil and demonic thought that tries to invade their mind be cast into the lake of fire never to arise again. I speak new thoughts, wholesome thoughts, and renewed thoughts. Thoughts of peace, love, joy, hope, ambition and growth overflow abundantly in their minds right now. I cast out doubt, fear, insecurities, hurt and pain right now.

What are the secrets of Life and How to prepare
For them.
Amos 5: 14-15 - The secret of life.
1. Seek good, & not evil that you may live; &
God shall be with you

2. Hate the evil

3. Love the good

4. Establish judgment in the gate

Amos 4: 12-13
PREPARE
1. Your self to meet God

2. A way for yourselves yourselves Dt. 19:3

3. Your heart 1Sam 7:3; 1Chr 29:18

4. Themsleves without fault Ps. 59:4

5. mercy & truth Ps 61:7

6 WORK Pr. 24:27

7. The way of the Lord Isa 40:3 Mt 3:9

8. The ways of the people Isa 62:10

_____

Joel 2:12-
Dt 4:29

~JoAnn~

From this day forth I speak nothing but thoughts of progress, elevation, and growth over your

mind. – Amen

Peering Outside The Box and Slaying The Inner Giant

Thinking outside the box requires that we change our mindset. We have to think like God would think and position our thinking away from negativity but towards positivity.
Turn these negative statements into positive statements thinking outside the box.

Negative	Positive
You will never get married	**God has an ordained husband for me; I am worthy to be a helpmate.**
You are overweight	
Your past is shameful	
You will never have children	
You are stupid	
You will never finish school	
Nobody likes me	
You are not worthy of a raise	
You will never finish what you started	
Nobody likes you	
You will always be a borrower	
You will never own anything	
You will never understand the Bible	
You are unattractive	
You have no purpose in life	

Psalm 68:19

Praise be to the Lord, to God our Savior, who daily bears our burdens.

LIVING LIFE STRAIGHT WITH NO CHASER

The 30 DAY CHALLENGE

SLAYING THE GIANT WITHIN

Day 2

Challenge: Releasing Toxic Baggage Out Of Your Life

One of the ways the giant tries to execute you is through your baggage. Baggage is defined as suitcases and other containers holding the belongings of people who are traveling. Also as ideas, beliefs, or practices retained from somebody's previous life experiences. The giant will try to attach heavy bags around your neck to choke out the things of God that are positioned on the inside of you. He will allow you to stuff excess hurt in suitcases in an attempt to hide them away. The enemy will also permit you to store them away in rolling suitcases, so you will be constantly reminded of them as you are rolling along on this journey called life. The giant will remind you of your baggage through baggage handlers. The baggage handlers are people, places and things that are attached to your life in a negative way. Baggage handlers have multiple roles. Baggage handlers are also mind distracters and vision killers. Their assignment is to keep you weighted down in the spirit.

I am reminded that when I go to deliver a package at the U.S. Post office they always ask me if my package contains any liquids, perishables, hazards or explosives. The reason they ask these questions because they must know what they are carrying or shipping so it won't be a problem for them or the other packages they are transporting. We must also adopt this same mentality and know what you are carrying spiritually, mentally, and psychologically. Many of you are carrying explosives daily and left untreated it will eventually explode. God showed me that explosives are hatred, hurt, pain, loss, discouragement, and so much more. So let me ask you a question. What is in your suitcase - bag? What are you carrying around in your suitcase – bag ?When I ask the question what is in your suitcase - bag I am not talking about that Samsonite Collection, Ciao Hardside Spinner Collection or that Travelpro Crew Luggage Collection. I am specifically talking about your spiritual, emotional and psychological bags. We all carry around baggage, rather it be a small change purse, a duffle bag or a large suitcase. Sadly, some of us have designer baggage we carry around. The problem is we just dress it up and carry it on our life shoulders trying to convince the world that we are exclusive and okay ,when the truth is we are tore up from the floor up.

Carrying around toxic baggage can be a hindrance in you fulfilling the purpose that God has for your life. Maya Angelou says that "Each of us has the right and the responsibility to assess the road which lies ahead and those over which we have traveled, and if the future road looms ominous or unpromising, and the road back uninviting-inviting, then we need to gather our resolve and carry only the necessary baggage, step off that road into another direction. If the new choice is also unpalatable, without embarrassment, we must be ready to change that choice as well." I fully agree with this God gives us free will to make decisions for our life and sometimes the choices we make hold us in bondage.

Carrying toxic baggage is unhealthy in all areas of your life .We sometimes want to believe that if we survived the hurt we are okay. If nobody knows about the baggage we are carrying, we are okay. If we don't carry a battle scare we are okay. The truth is that is all a lie. Baggage is bad! Just like baggage, toxins are also bad for us. Anything that is toxic means it contains poison or toxin. A toxin is described as something that can cause serious harm or death. When you continue to carry around the toxic baggage you are living a slow and painful death. Carrying toxic baggage is like inhaling carbon monoxide. With carbon monoxide it is odorless but deadly. It will sneak up on you and kill you.

The way the toxins operate in our life is very much like the enemy. It slowly kills your dreams, steals your purpose and destroys the destiny God has purposed for your life. Although we all carry baggage, the most common form of baggage is emotional baggage. Emotional baggage is defined as the feelings you have about your past and the things that have happened to you, which often have a negative effect on your behavior and attitudes. When you don't deal with your emotional baggage, you may turn to food, alcohol, work, money- spending, sex, or drugs. I will share my own testimony. As a result of me not dealing with my emotional baggage it affected me in my relationships. I approached each relationship as the victim and allowed negative people to siege my joy, peace and happiness. It wasn't until I renewed my relationship with God in 1990that I was able to put down my suitcase of sadness and replace it with a backpack of blessings.

When you are carrying around toxic baggage it begins to make you feel forsaken. The word says in Psalm 9:9-19 that The Lord will be a refuge for the oppressed, a refuge in times of trouble. And they that know thy name will put their trust in thee. For thou Lord hasn't not forsaken them that seek thee.

Unloading Your Toxins and Slaying The Inner Giant

Make a list of all of the toxins that you need to unpack from that suitcase. Hurt, Shame, Pain, Relationships, and etc.

1)

2)

3)

4)

5)

6)

7)

8)

9)

10)

11)

12)

13)

14)

15)

16)

17)

Healthy Affirmations For Healing – Slaying The Inner Giant

Place these affirmations on index cards and read them aloud. Place them in places you can see them daily. Let these affirmations become a part of your daily life.

With my heart open to God's renovating love, I accept my healing now.

❖

I am emotionally healthy and psychologically strong. I am complete with God's healing,

energizing presence in my life.

❖

I am created in the image of God, highly blessed with an abundance of strength and wholeness.

❖

The power of God withstands and exalts me with perfect emotional health.

❖

Philippians 4:8

"Finally, brothers, whatever is true, whatever is honorable, whatever is just, whatever is pure, whatever is lovely, whatever is commendable, if there is any excellence, if there is anything worthy of praise, think about these things."

LIVING LIFE STRAIGHT WITH NO CHASER

The 30 DAY CHALLENGE

SLAYING THE GIANT WITHIN

Day 3

Challenge: Don't Accept Negativity from Others

Negativity has a purpose; it seeks to generate fear and insecurity in the life of Gods people.

Negativity is just like that giant. It comes to intimidate and manipulate us into not going forth in

the things that we know will bring us blessings and contentment

Negativity also yanks on our personal fears and tries to hinder us from operating in our ordained

gifts. Negativity serves as a red light jolting us from moving forward in the things of God.

Negativity is defined as expressing, containing, or consisting of a negation, refusal, or denial

about a specific matter.

When we think of negativity we are mostly reminded of negative people and the undesirable

energy they put off into the atmosphere. This quote helps me to understand the spirit of

negativity. I will share it with you .Negativity pulls away energy. If part of the negativity stems from your attitude or perspective, commit yourself at the beginning of each day and each activity to find something positive in yourself and in others around you. If the people around you are negative you can't change this. Either remove yourself from the situation or view it simply as one obstacle you face in pursuing your own potential. Stay focused on your own goals and makes the best of the situation. - **TERRY ORLICK, Embracing Your Potential.**

The line of attack we must take against the enemy, is the responsibility of not letting others negativity evade our personal space in life. We must be aware that there are people whose sole mission is to creep into our lives and cause discord .We have to discontinue them on their destructive path. The way to do that is when they call you on the phone with negative conversation or approach you with undesirable conversation tell them wrong number. Proverb 15:1, 2 reminds us that a soft answer turneth away wrath: but grievous words stirs up anger. The tongue of the wise useth knowledge aright: but the mouth of fools poureth out foolishness.

We must guard our life like the Secret Service guards the President. We are the gate keepers to our mind, body and soul. We can't allow everyone access. Everyone doesn't have good intentions. There are many people who thrive off of negativity and will do whatever the devil tells them they are big and bold enough to do.

I have found that People are so quick to want to deposit negativity into your life, but we have to be quicker at rebuking it and not accepting these snippets of doubt and hatred into our life. 1

Peter 5:8 tells us - Be sober, be vigilant; because your adversary the devil is like a roaring lion, walketh about, seeking whom he may devour.

Negativity is like a cancer it eats away at your spiritual well-being. Negativity is like a gateway drug to other sinful behaviors. Be cautious who you allow to speak into or over your life. Our ear gate is the entrance to our mind and our mind the path to our heart .The enemy is the author of confusion. He thrives when dissension surfaces in your life. It is very important that we speak life over our own life. We have to be confident in who we are in Christ. When we are spiritually confident and negativity surfaces we can speak the truth to the enemy and make him flee.

I know throughout my life I heard a lot of negative words projected towards me but I thank God I didn't let them pierce my spirit and fester. I had a middle school teacher to tell me that I was never going to be anything and implied that I would work at a fast food restaurant because I lacked potential to do anything else. I am here to say fast food was never my profession. The negativity she hurled at me encouraged me to be successful as an author, mother, and social service worker and visionary. I even had negativity to come at me from people in my life that I loved and trusted. I have had men in my life say, I was too fat, to dark, and too naïve but I thank God He, meaning Jesus Christ said I was made in his image and that made me good enough.

Thank God I have a renewed mind and know myself worth. Today I challenge you to work on stopping people and circumstances from speaking into your life negatively. I challenge you to look at yourself in the mirror every day and see something beautiful within yourself. I challenge you to speak over your life and declare that you are not the things hurled at you from childhood;

you are not the mistakes you made in your young adult years. You are not those failed

relationships or other mistakes you made along the way. I challenge you to change your focus

and know that change will occur once you decide to change it with God's help. Change will

come when you decide to slay the giant within.

Matthew 16:25

For whosoever will save his life shall lose it, and whosoever loses his life for my sake will find it.

LIVING LIFE STRAIGHT WITH NO CHASER

The 30 DAY CHALLENGE

SLAYING THE GIANT WITHIN

Day 4

Challenge: Close That Door

God's word says he is the Alpha and the Omega, this means he is the beginning and the end. He had to endure many different circumstances before he had to close the chapter on death. .

Everything that has a beginning also must have an end. There can be no birth without conception; there can be no fire without a flame. There is no life without death. When we come into this world nobody should realistically think that they will live forever. For every door open it must be closed. The consequence for keeping doors open that are intended to be closed can attract the wrong things to come in and severely affect the atmosphere in your life.

On this journey that we are on, there will be many experiences where we must have closure on. There will be certain people, place and things. There will be people that we may have to close the door on. There will be places we can no longer visit, and there will be things, habits and lifestyle choices we have to just view from our rear view mirror.

When God closes a door we have to leave it shut. I believe God closes doors in our life because he knows that with that door staying open it can cause many problems in our life. God will always give you a warning on doors that need to be closed. The word tells us in Mark 8:15

(NIV) "Be careful," Jesus warned them. "Watch out for the yeast of the Pharisees and that of

Herod." Warning comes before destruction.

Although warning is upon us, many go back and kick the door open to get back into their life of

sin because it is comfortable. The Lord is trying to close that door to poverty but you keep

playing lotto. He is trying to close the door to homosexuality but you refuse to lose soul ties. He

is trying to close that door to your childhood hurt but you refuse to give up the victim role. He is

trying to send you a husband but you won't release that feeling of not being good enough and

willingness to submit. Whatever door you are leaving open, I command you to close it right now

in the name of Jesus. What door do you need to close in your life today?

While some can close the door, others are going to have to slam the Door! Take if off its hinges,

Just DONT GO BACK IN! Going back in that door can be your one way ticket to destruction

and nothing is worth spending eternity in misery. Last week I had to close the door on a

relationship that needed to be closed months ago but out of flesh I allowed that door to remain

open. It was a challenge but all my fears and insecurities flared up at once and left me feeling

isolated. Closing that door meant that I was going to have to release all the memories,

experiences, good times and bad out of my spirit. Closing that door meant I no longer would

have an emotional safety net to fall on when I needed it. Closing that door was painful and

stressful however, I needed to close the door to move into the things of God. I had to make a choice and I chose closure. As a result of my obedience, I am looking for God's heavenly doors to swing open and bless me. God will reward those that diligently seek him and his ways.

There is POWER in releasing something to get something. Closure is hard but it's a must for those who are following after the heartbeat of Jesus.

Closure Letter and Slaying The Inner Giant

Write a letter to the door that you have to close. Share why it must be closed, the consequences

of keeping it open and what you hope to accomplish of having that door closed.

Date

Dear _____,

2 John 1:2

❖

Because of the truth, this lives in us and will be with us forever

LIVING LIFE STRAIGHT WITH NO CHASER

The 30 DAY CHALLENGE

SLAYING THE GIANT WITHIN

Day 5

Challenge: Facing Truth

"I found power in accepting the truth of who I am. It may not be a truth that others can accept, but I cannot live any other way. How would it be to live a lie every minute of your life?"

— Alison Goodman, Eon: Dragoneye Reborn

Goliath the giant was hiding the truth from David. He wanted David to believe that he was invincible. He wanted David to think he was the strongest beast around. He wanted David to think that nobody could slay him. During these times the enemy uses the same tactics.

When we can face the truth about ourselves and our circumstances we can then live a life that has no set boundaries. Loving ourselves has the greatest defeat in human time. As humans we are always in search of the truth. Society has done a poor job of defining how we are supposed to live and love. Nobody teaches us the importance of loving ourselves they emphasize the importance of loving others. . Yes, the Bible tells us to love our neighbors as ourselves and it is the number one commandment but I do believe that God also want us to love ourselves.

Today is "FACE THE TRUTH ". We must face truth and deal with the inner demons that reside within us. We must deal with the fear, failures, and faults that linger in our life before we can forge ahead. Nobody knows you like you. Be true to yourself and seek the resources you need to become a better you. There is a Solution to every problem. Ask God to help you. Jeremiah 33:3 tells us to call unto him and he will answer. There is no need to live life in torment. When you can have triumph over the giant that is blocking your blessings. Take Control over your destiny and decide to live. Evict those giants that have over stayed their welcome in your life.

Facing the Truth

Before I realized who I was in Christ I didn't see myself as an attractive, smart, educated, God fearing woman. I had allowed the enemy to tell me that I was fat, ugly, worthless, to short, not smart enough and many other things. When it dawned on me that the enemy was a liar and there was no truth in him; I begin to see the beauty within myself. I begin to see that my smile was beautiful and my hair wasn't as nappy as I had been told during my childhood. I realized I was fearfully and wonderfully made in God's image. After much prayer and support from people that loved me. I began to see that I had qualities that other people appreciated and it wasn't just my body but my mind was valuable too. What are some of the lies that the enemy has told you?

Write down the things the enemy told you that you later found out was a lie.

Lies – Slaying The Inner Giant

1)

2)

3)

4)

5)

6)

7)

8)

9)

10)

11)

12)

13)

14)

15)

Psalm 139:23-24

❖

Search me , O God , and know my heart: try me , and know my

thoughts: And see if there be any wicked way in me , and lead me in

the way everlasting .

LIVING LIFE STRAIGHT WITH NO CHASER

The 30 DAY CHALLENGE

SLAYING THE GIANT WITHIN

Day 6

Challenge: Becoming Transparent

The word for today is TAKE THE MASK OFF! We need to just be real with God and take the

mask off. He already knows our strengths and weaknesses; he already knows our hurt and pain.

He already knows our secret places and things. We have to uncover the things that hold us back

from serving God completely. We have to speak them out of our mouth and eject them out of our

heart. We have to admit we are sick and desire to get well. TAKE THE MASK OFF. We have to

let those wounds heal; we have to forgive people we feel have hurt us. We must repent for the

things we know are wrong. We have to stop acting like we are okay when we are tore up from

the floor up, when we have issues that need tissues. Are you willing to take the mask off and

walk naked before the Lord? The benefits of taking off the mask is allowing the Holy Spirit to

heal you from the inside out and giving you a new face to present to the world. Ladies and

gentlemen lets be real with God. We have to stop trying to please the world with a facade. We

have to admit our faults and just say I am tired of wearing this mask, take me as I am. We have

to UNDRESS our MESS!!!! Does anybody feel me? Is anybody torn up like me? When I say I

am torn up, I mean I had a lot of masks on. I was a people pleaser and wore the mask of trying to fit in and feel accepted. This mask was one I had to quickly let go because I had to quickly realize that regardless of how much you do for people it will never be enough. During my desire to please others I would go all out of my way financially and emotionally to make sure others had the things they needed when I knew I could not afford it. I usually did this with men I was in intimate partner relationships with. I would make sure they had all the things they needed. I realized that I was trying to be accepted by these men. I was sacrificing my finances to make sure they were happy. God showed me that as long as I was doing for them they were happy and it brought me happiness also but in an unhealthy way .However, when the money was gone they were to and I was left feeling depleted and used. My mask after this experience was pretending to be happy at the expenses of others being happy.

When we strive to please others instead of pleasing God, we are hiding behind a dangerous mask. God wants us to be transparent and be ourselves instead of being who others want us to be. After pulling that people pleasing mask off, I found me. I discovered that I was just fine the way I was and I didn't need man's approval after all. It was not an easy journey to go through. It was a nasty habit that needed to be broken. Apart of breaking free, I had to allow God to sever those strong ties that was holding me captives to others. The mask of this lonely little girl craving acceptance had to be uncovered. I wanted to hide that part of my life. Keeping the mask on helped me to hide the hurt and rejection that I had been feeling for years. The real hurt was wanting to feel the acceptance of my biological father who was AWOL in my life. The feeling was not feeling connected to a mother who I felt never showed me the type of love I desired. I

came to grips with the fact that nobody was responsible for the way I was accepting how I felt

but me.

Transparent: What does that mean?

Being Transparent and Slaying The Inner Giant

Why is it hard for you to be transparent?

What are you some of the barriers you face in exposing some of your hurt and pain? What are

the things that stand in the way of you being healed, set free and delivered?

Genesis 2:7

Then the Lord God formed a man from the dust of the ground and

breathed into his nostrils the breath of life, and the man became a

living being.

LIVING LIFE STRAIGHT WITH NO CHASER

The 30 DAY CHALLENGE

SLAYING THE GIANT WITHIN

Day 7

Challenge: Inhale, Exhale

Focusing on the act of breathing clears the mind of all daily distractions and clears our energy enabling us to better connect with the Spirit within. ~Author Unknown

When we can better connect with the act of breathing it clears our mind away from the foreign deity that tries to attach themselves to us from the outer corners of the world. When God breathed life into man it was attached to purpose. The reason we as humans breathe is to ultimately have breath in our bodies to serve our God. I believe when we inhale and exhale we are subconsciously inviting in the Holy Spirit to dwell within us.

The word for today is breathe. To breathe is to take in air, to push out substances of breath , to smell something , to allow air through your lungs, to live, to pause and rest , to wait gently and to breathe new life into something or to bring new energy or vigor to something.

In order to have a full communion with God we must release some of the anxieties that have built up in our life. You have to clear out the fog and toxins that has confined your ability to breathe. Breathe, exhale and enjoy the fullness of the Lord. Breathe and escape from the snares of the enemy. Appreciate the things that God has presented to you. Breathe slowly and wisely stop being so congested by the world's antics and evil devices.

Separate yourself from the foolishness that desires to make you become asthmatic in the spirit. In the natural when a person is asthmatic they have trouble with increased cough, wheezing with physical activity, tiredness, it decreases your peak expiratory flow, causes restless sleep, and worsens allergy symptoms. The same things happen spiritually when we don't take the time to breathe properly in the things of God and allow the freshness of God's word and spirit to enter our temple. The enemy desires to cut off your life source and stop you from breathing in the freshness of his love. Decide today to breath and welcome in the fresh aroma that God has given you. There may be people, places and things that are consuming too much of your spiritual air causing you to be short of breath. I encourage you to run to the source of life and that is Jesus Christ. The one thing that kept me from breathing the fresh air of God was unforgiveness. I was going through life refusing to forgive others that had hurt me. I wanted to hold on to the unforgiveness because I was in a comfortable spot. Once I realized that the forgiveness was not for the other person but more so for me, I began to see how God was breathing his fresh breath on me to be free from the bondages of others. Whatever you are going through you can be free. Allow God to breathe on you. Let him inhale and exhale in areas of your life that need healing and deliverance power.

Breathing Again and Slaying The Inner Giant

1. What kinds of things are cutting off your spiritual life supply?

A)

B)

C)

D)

2. What would it take for you to breathe again?

A)

B)

C)

D)

Psalm 142:5

I cry to you, Lord; I say, "You are my refuge, my portion in the land

of the living."

LIVING LIFE STRAIGHT WITH NO CHASER

The 30 DAY CHALLENGE

SLAYING THE GIANT WITHIN

Day 8

Challenge: Decide to Live!

There was a young lady in her early 30's who was diagnosed with cervical cancer and she was given 3 months to live by her doctor. She came home and spoke with her husband of 10 years and said "I have cancer and I am going to die. I can do two things I can LIVE or I can DIE. Her husband was shocked. He was looking for her to breakdown and cry but she just threw her purse on the couch and said, "I have decided to LIVE". After dinner, very quietly she made a list of places she wanted to travel, foods from other cultures she wanted to experience, she even decided she wanted to meet friends from her Face Book friends list that she had never seen in person. She called her closet family members. She wanted to share this with them. Knowing she would only have 3 months to live, she withdrew all her earthly savings and sold her most precious jewels and antiques. With her husband and family members in tow, she sought out to LIVE before her expiration date. She checked off all the beautiful places she had seen and the wonderful food she partook of. She was in awe to find all her Face Book friends were as lovely as she had imagined. While on this journey she realized that she had forgotten about her circumstances because she was living. One day while asleep she had a dream that she had a baby. She said how this could be. She shared this with her husband and he said he had dreamt the same thing. After 2 ½ months on the road she knew it was time to return home and face her death. Through all of this she kept telling herself that she was destined to live and not die.

She went for her follow up appointment with the doctor to have her levels done and to check her blood work, to find out that she was cancer free and pregnant. This shows that when you decide to live, God will live through you and grant you the desires of your heart.

The words for today is live life and don't let life live you. If we go through life just accepting anything we lose sight of our purpose and are unable to regain our true focus. We tend to forget that life is much more than going to work, church, the gym and home. In order to fully benefit from the joys of life we have to add a little more flavor to our existence. Enjoy nature, spend time with positive family and friends, enjoy some of your childhood games and pleasures, invest in a vacation to another city, state or country, dance in the rain, do something adventurous.

Life was meant to be enjoyed and not envied. We have to stop thinking that just because we are Christians we cannot have a good time. We are supposed to laugh and have joy in our hearts. We are supposed to surround ourselves with people who create positive energy for us to enjoy.

Stop letting life live you, thinking you can't do certain things. You can do all things through Christ Jesus who strengthens you. Smile more and someone will smile back at you. Give someone a hug and, you will be embraced by love. Sow a seed into someone's life and your harvest will be plenteous.

I have decided I am going to live my life more carefree. My children are older there is nothing stopping me from living life. I have a flexible job, no husband right now to adjust my schedule for. I am just going to don't worry and be happy! There are millions of foods I haven't tired, a trillion places I haven't

explored, billions of people I haven't met. There is so much more and I am ready for it. Are you?

Live or Die Survey- Slaying The Inner Giant

If you were advised that you had 3 months to live would you give up and die, or would you decide to live? Here is your 90 day bucket list, tell me what you would do.

Where would you go to visit?

Who would you spend time with and why?

What would you do that is exciting?

Name something adventurous you would do?

Would you spend more time with family or friends?

Would you spend more time with God?

Would you travel?

Would you start that hobby you always wanted to do?

After completing this self-survey, survey your life and ask yourself how come you are not doing these things now. What is stopping you from fulfilling the things on this list and why. Remember you have to live life. Don't let life live you.

Psalm 32:1-2

Happy is the person whose sins are forgiven, whose wrongs are pardoned. Happy is the person whom the Lord does not consider guilty in whom there is nothing false.

LIVING LIFE STRAIGHT WITH NO CHASER

The 30 DAY CHALLENGE

SLAYING THE GIANT WITHIN

Day 9

Challenge: Forgiveness

I am so glad that God loves us enough to forgive us of our many conscious and unconscious sins. There was a time in my life that I was extremely angry with a family member. I was angry because I felt this person did not protect me when I was a child. I was angry because for many years I had fought emotionally to make this person love me. I was angry because I thought this person should have been more involved in my life. I was angry because this person didn't show me the type of love that I felt I deserved. I was hurt, felt abandoned, and often felt like the black sheep of the family because of the circumstances. In my heart I decided to just hate this person and vowed to never let the back into my life. After years into my adulthood, God started to work on my heart and showed me that I had to forgive. The process of forgiving was not an easy process for me. I thought that forgiving this person symbolized that the person was right and I was wrong. I felt like forgiving this person would make me vulnerable for future hurt from others. It wasn't until I let the Lord into my heart that I realized that forgives wasn't for me but more so for the other person. I had to release this pain. I had to let the pain go so I could be free from the giants grip.

I remember getting an opportunity to talk to this person in person. I felt like the weight of the world was being released from my life. I felt like the stone was being rolled away from my grave of affliction. It wasn't until I let go that God begin to let me heal. I am reminded of Mark 11:25 that say, when you are praying, if you are angry with someone, forgive him so that your Father in Heaven will also forgive your sins. I need my sins to be forgiven, because I then realized I was not without sin. I want you to think about that person you have not forgiven. I want you to accept the fact that until you forgive them you will not be free to live the life that God has ordained for you. All the pain and stress your feeling behind this person is attached to you and that person could have moved on and not thinking about you or the situation any longer. We give people control when we don't release them .We give them power when we don't deal with the situation. We have to learn to let go and not allow the enemy to convince us to simmer in the hatred that surrounds unforgiveness. We must slay the giant within. We must get our slingshots out and aim at the problem then release all the pain

The other side of forgiveness is that we have to ask others for forgiveness that we have wronged in our life. 1 John 1:9 says but if we confess our sins he will forgive our sins because we can trust God to do what is right. He will cleanse us from all the wrongs we have done. Forgiveness is serious business. We can't please God if we don't forgive others or accept others apologizes when they ask for forgiveness. If you have the opportunity to forgive someone please do. I cannot stress this enough. Colossians 3:13 reminds us that we are to get along with each other, and forgive each other. If someone does wrong to you, forgive that person because the Lord forgave you. There was a catchy phrase that was said a few years ago. It was "W.W.J.D.? " Ask yourself that same question the next time you are indecisive about forgiving someone.

The first step to getting it right is discussing the issue. Isaiah 1:18 says The Lord says, "Come, let us talk about these things. Though your sins are like scarlet, they can be as white as snow. Though your sins are deep red, they can be white as wool. "Take your concerns to the Lord and the other person and leave it there.

Reflect on this Scripture –Slaying The Inner Giant

What does this scripture say to you?

Colossians 2:13

When you were spiritually dead because of your sin and because you were not free from the

power of your sinful self, God made you alive with Christ, and he forgave all our sins.

LIVING LIFE STRAIGHT WITH NO CHASER

The 30 DAY CHALLENGE

SLAYING THE GIANT WITHIN

Day 10

Challenge: Let Go and Let God- Stop Pretending

I remember when I was struggling financially. I had two young children that were depending on me to have it all together. My world was crumbling down all around me and I was too embarrassed to ask my family or true friends for financial support. I was walking around pretending like everything was okay. I had mastered the art of pretending. I would dress myself up and pretend like everything was okay. My thought was, if I just dressed the part nobody would notice. I tried to smile but often times all I would get were tears that ran down my face. I would try to pretend that nothing bothered me but in reality I was dying a slow and painful death internally. Pretending will cause you to make poor decisions in life and the consequences for those choices can sometimes be detrimental to your spiritual and physical health. God is willing to see us through. We have to just trust him 24-7. We also have to stop pretending when we are emotionally wounded and hurt.

We can't just brush that hurt under the rug and forget about it. We have to expose the hurt and heal from the inside out. Perhaps we should seek professional and or spiritual counsel. Stop suffering in your cave alone.

The word for today is STOP PRETENDING. Stop pretending you are okay when you know the world is falling down on you on every side of you like boulders of bricks during a scheduled demolition. Stop trying to be so durable when you know you are faint and weak. Stop saying you don't need help when you know within you are a nervous wreck. Stop hindering people from blessing you when you know you asked God for a miracle. My brothers and Sisters just stop pretending.

As Christians we sometimes feel like we have to be strong all the time. Being weak is okay, because when we are weak he is resilient. He told us he would be our burden bearer so, we can put down all those barrels, and barrels of problematic bricks and just give it entirely to him.

When you feel overwhelmed and pretending is the only option. I advise you to reach out to other saints who can inspire you and pray you through. You don't have to pretend. You don't have to keep your wonder women or Bat man cape on and pretend you are tough all the time. I know I had some very weak moments in my forty plus years and often I would lay in my bed as if I would die. I felt if I revealed my real problems that people would say I was crazy and weak, so I suffered in silence.

We must be real and stop pretending. Stop pretending that all your bills are paid and you don't get collection calls. Stop pretending your husband or wife is perfect or pretend your kids are little angel's .We all struggle with something. Stop pretending. Get out of LaLa land. The easy bake oven cannot make a wedding cake, the Barbie and Ken house, you cannot live in, the dress up clothes you have outgrown, let's move out of fantasy land into faith land . We have to stop pretending. I am not saying don't dream just stop fooling yourself. Your situation is what it is until God changes your situation.

Pretending has NO Value in Your Life- Slaying The Inner Giant

1. When did you realize that pretending everything was okay seemed better than facing the truth head on?

2. What age were you when you start pretending? What situation in your life made pretending comfortable?

3. What is your biggest fear? What is that one thing you are afraid people will find out?

Matthew 16:9

I will give you the keys of the Kingdom of Heaven, and whatever you bind on earth shall be bound in Heaven, and whatever you loose on earth shall be loosed in Heaven.

LIVING LIFE STRAIGHT WITH NO CHASER

The 30 DAY CHALLENGE

SLAYING THE GIANT WITHIN

Day 11

Challenge: Unlocking your Destiny

The seven deadly sins provide keys to understanding our faults and the actions that result, and a framework for self-knowledge. If we understood how they factor into who we have become, we would understand much more about ourselves and our effect on others.

- **Author Unknown**

The word for today is KEYS. There are certain keys that will open certain doors in your life. The key that open your house door will not be the same key that cranks up your car. Find that special key that will open the gifts that God has imparted into you. Activate that spiritual ignition on the inside of you with the key ingredients that God has given you. The key to your purpose is Jesus Christ. Take your extra set of keys back from the devil and get your heart, mind, body and soul re-keyed. Don't give out anymore spares keys unless they are supporting you with Emotional, Spiritual, Psychological, and Financial support. I advise you not to give away your valuables. We sometimes give away keys to our heart before people are eligible to receive it. We take into account that everyone has our best interest at heart and in reality this is so far from the truth. People should have to earn our heart keys. This isn't something we should so freely give away.

The word tells us in Proverbs 4:23 Above all else, guard your heart, for everything you do flows from it. This word is truly signature statements for everyone to ponder on .Here are a few Spiritual Keys to meditate on today.

K- Keep yourself covered at all times. Through the blood, we are brought into the very presence of God. Psalm 91 is the most familiar passage about the protection and covering from God. In the scripture the psalmist declares that the Lord is a refuge and harbor of safety, it explains He protects us from evil traps and plagues. This assurance can help us guard our hearts from fear. The beauty of this scripture is that he also promises that angels will protect us.

E- Explore your options before making carnal choices. Proverbs 4:7 tells us, Wisdom is the principal thing; therefore get wisdom: and with all thy getting get an understanding. When we have a know -it -all spirit we may make hasty decisions that will eventually lead to our own ruin. We have to explore the word of God and see what he says about our decisions and consult him first and foremost. Always remember that God has a plan and without him and his plan we will surely fail.

Y- Yes! Always give God a YES! Regardless of how things look in the natural. Seek Gods approval with a yes in your spirit. A Yes is what moves God to usher in the things that your heart desires. A Yes will move mountains. A Yes will break chains, A Yes will move hurdles out of your way. A Yes will propel your none to plenty. All God want is a YES

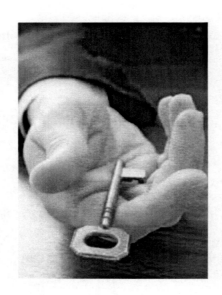

The Key is in your hand. What are you going to do with it?

Slaying The Inner Giant

*

*

*

Romans 5:8

❖

But God shows his great love for us in this ways: Christ died

for us while were still sinners

LIVING LIFE STRAIGHT WITH NO CHASER

The 30 DAY CHALLENGE

SLAYING THE GIANT WITHIN

Day 12

Challenge: Loving Unconditionally

God loves you just the way you are, but He refuses to leave you that way. He wants

you to be just like Jesus. – Max Lucado

The word for today is LOVE... I would say LOVE others like you love yourself but some of us don't even love ourselves. I was thinking okay, well love each other like you love God but we fall short there also. Love is one of Gods greatest commandments and this is all that he requires of us to do. We have to set aside our differences and allow God to help us to walk in Godly Love. Walking in Godly love is forgiving one another, being our brother and sisters keeper, carrying one another's burdens, feeding each other physically, emotionally, psychologically and spiritually, sharing our testimonies and etc.

When we say that we love one another we have to follow it with ACTION. Love is an action word. We have to be LOVE SUPER HEROS and we have to leap from tall buildings to help our brothers and sisters, come off our high horses and meeting people where they are spiritually and naturally. We have to fly through the air, meaning we have to send prayers up and glide them into heaven's door. When we see destruction heading towards our brothers and sister we have to derail the situation with prayer, fasting and supplication. Remember, Love is an Action word. We have souls to save and the only way we are going to be able to do that is by showing LOVE. Go out and love somebody today. Offer a quick wave, a friendly smile, a kind hand , give some something to eat, pray with someone, sow a seed, visit the prison, volunteer at a school. Do something constructive; put your love to work.

Supportive Love Scriptures

What Does these Scriptures Mean to You?

Slaying The Inner Giant

Jeremiah 31:3 And from far away the Lord appeared to his people and said, "I love you people with a love that will last forever. " That is why I have continued showing you kindness"

Thoughts:

Hosea 2:19   And I will make you my promised bride forever. I will be good and fair, I will show you my love and mercy.

Thoughts:

James 4:7

Submit yourselves therefore to God. Resist the devil,

and he will flee from you.

LIVING LIFE STRAIGHT WITH NO CHASER

The 30 DAY CHALLENGE

SLAYING THE GIANT WITHIN

Day 13

Challenge: Submission

What is Submission?

The act of submitting, yielding, or surrendering; the quality or condition of being submissive; resignation; obedience; meekness; the act of submitting something to.

HAVE YOU EVER BEEN LEFT AT THE ALTAR? I have .No; I am NOT talking about the altar to get married but to submit myself before God in prayer.

There have been times when I needed to stay a little bit longer to cleanse my soul and spend a little bit more time with my father. It's okay to be left there. Don't worry if the choir has stop singing, or the ushers are still hovering over your back. Don't worry if the tears are streaming down your face, or the preacher has started to move on with service. You stay right there until you have emptied yourself out and gotten what you came there for. The Church is a hospital and it is for "Spiritually Sick" people. You wouldn't go to the hospital with a physical illness and leave before the doctor at least saw you. God is a healer of all our infirmities. Stay right there, and get your breakthrough. Don't worry about what people are going to say as you are walking back to your seat. Don't worry about the stares and glares. Get yours! There is healing at the altar. Submission is good for the soul.

Let's look at the woman who had the issue of blood. She was in a position to submit herself to God. She was in a place where it didn't matter who saw her stretching out her hand for a touch of his garment. She was just trying to be made whole. She knew that submitting to him was going to free her from the frailties that were upon her. She wasn't caring how her weave was looking or how her nails were polished. She was more concerned with being made whole. She was on a spiritual assignment and she had one thing on her mind. That one thing was deliverance.

If we know that submission is or what is required, why won't we submit to God? Fear is the number one reason we do not submit wholeheartedly. We are afraid to give up control. Many of us are control freaks and would rather work it out ourselves than allow God to arbitrate and show himself mighty. We have a master plan and feel the only way it can be achieved is if we do it ourselves. We are petrified to hand it over to the one that created us. Fear paralyzes your ability to think clearly. Fear subjects you to sin. Fear obstructs your view from the truth. Fear leads you down a path of unrighteousness. Fear stands at your gate of purpose and barricades your entry into abundance. Fear is the catalyst to failure and demise. Fear hinders your ability to connect with the necessary resources you need to be whole and complete. When I was in college; I had a huge fear of passing the CLAST test, the math section was the part that really scared me. I was afraid to even deal with anything that pertained to math. I avoided classes that required that I use any form of mathematical concepts. It wasn't until I decided to conquer that fear that math became clearer and clearer to me. When the anxieties would come, I would say to myself, I can do all things through Christ Jesus. After surrendering my fears, things began to get a lot better for me. I am happy to say I passed the CLAST test and took several classes like statistics that involved lots of logic and numbers and passed with flying colors. It was when I released the fear and submitted to God for help I was able to move forward.

Ponder on this scripture .**James 4:7 - Submit yourselves therefore to God. Resist the devil, and he will flee from you.** If we could build on this scripture, our life will reflect a life of submission.

Although I know submitting is not easy, it is essential in building a solid relationship with God. God loves his child to live a life of obedience. 1 Samuel 15:22 says "Hath the Lord as great delight in burnt offerings and sacrifices as in obeying the voice of the Lord? Behold, to obey is better than sacrifice, and to hearken than the fat of rams. This is confirmation that God longs for us to submit. Are you willing to submit today? The choice is yours.

Submission 101- Slaying The Inner Giant

What are your views on submission?

What have you been taught about submission?

Do you feel that you submit to authority without debate? Explain

Do you think the scripture about wives / husbands submitting to one another is historic in the society we live in?

Psalm 37:34

Wait for the Lord and keep his way, and he will exalt you to inherit

the land: you will look on when the wicked are cut off.

LIVING LIFE STRAIGHT WITH NO CHASER

The 30 DAY CHALLENGE

SLAYING THE GIANT WITHIN

Day 14

Challenge: Expectation

I wonder how many people were betting against David and were rooting for Goliath. Many were probably expecting Goliath to tear little old David to pieces. Many were probably expecting David to just surrender so they would have easily collected on their bets. It is so hard when everyone is expecting you to lose. When no one believes that you should receive a harvest for the hard work you have sown. What others did not know is that David had sown some spiritual seeds and God was going to let him reap that day.

The word for today is Get your Spiritual deposit slip out. The Lord is telling me to tell his people to GET THEIR DEPOSIT SLIP OUT. He has heard your pleas for help. He has seen your watery eyes, he has seen the mistreatment you have endured and he is on the way. He knows we all need a deposit of the Holy Spirit in our life. He knows we are suffering in our finances, he knows our children are being wayward, he knows our significant others are going astray, he knows our jobs are being threatened, he knows our faith is growing faint. He knows our dreams are growing dimmer, he knows our hearts have been shattered; He knows our health is not up to par. The message he has sent is Get your Spiritual deposit slip out .YES, he is about to deposit a NEW thing in our life. He says the faith account you once had open will not be able to receive that deposit that he has in store for you, so he is closing that account and making you a faith account holder in the Bank of Faith international, you can make transactions anywhere in the world with this account. He says that he is cleaning out that old account because it was not drawing any interest. He said with this new account you will accumulate interest and the dividends will be beneficial to your life.

The devil want us to keep going to pay day loans (people, places and things), and loaning out our soul for a hefty surcharge but tell that devil you now have an account and it is secured. Our life is secure in Jesus. God is ready to deposit into your faith account all the things you have sown. The word tells us we will reap what we have sown and I am a witness I have sown my share of seeds in the kingdom and into Gods people and I am ready to reap my harvest. I got my deposit slip out and I am ready. I use to depend on others to make a deposit into my life but they were all making the wrong types of deposits. Depositing lies, hate, hurt, pain, discord and etc. After experiencing so much pain, I now know that God is my resource. He is my Jehovah Jirah, My provider.

I got my deposit slip out and I am ready for my account to register, blessed, anointed, and secure in Jesus, with no more overdrawn charges. Anybody with me? , With Jesus all our charges have been paid. Thank you Jesus.

In order to get your deposit you must sign up for direct deposit. You must give the Holy Spirit your rotating number and heavenly account number. There is no way to receive besides being on the payroll of the heavenly father.

Many say they are ready to receive but are unwilling to release anything from their hands or heart. The word tells us in Galatians 6:7-8: "Be not deceived; God is not mocked: for whatsoever a man soweth, that shall he also reap. For he that soweth to his flesh shall of the flesh reap corruption; but he that soweth to the Spirit shall of the Spirit reap life everlasting."

If we sow good we shall reap good. If we sow grudgingly we will reap grudgingly. God is faithful to his word.

We have to have the mindset like a farmer. We have to till our ground, plant a seed, water it, fertilize it and watch it grow. While waiting for your deposit you have to speak life over your crop.

I have never seen a farmer plant seeds and neglect it and expect a harvest. I leave you with a question how will you prepare for your harvest?

Expect the Great- Slaying The Inner Giant

What crop are you spiritually planting?

What spiritual tools are you going to need to get a full harvest?

What is your strategy for if your crop is attacked by unexpected circumstances?

Who are you going to share your crop with? Where will you sow?

Romans 8:28

And we know that God causes all things to work together for good to those who love God, to those who are called according to His purpose.

LIVING LIFE STRAIGHT WITH NO CHASER

The 30 DAY CHALLENGE

SLAYING THE GIANT WITHIN

Day 15

Challenge: Closure

David could have easily closed the chapter on this story and cowardly laid down and let Goliath just rip him to pieces. The story of David and Goliath would have had a totally different meaning to us today .David I believe was looking at the outcome and not the opponent. When God is closing a chapter in our life we must look at where God is taking us versus where we have been. The word for today is CLOSURE. We have to close the door on some offensive people, corrupt places and contaminated things. When God closes a door we have to learn to leave it shut. The difficulties we have are we go back and kick the door open to get back in. Why do we do that? , IT IS BECAUSE WE ARE UNCOMFORTABLE WITH THE UNKNOWN. What door do you need God to close in your life today? Is it a person God told you to let go, is it a habit, is it a job, is it a sin, is it a place you need to stop going. Whatever it is close the door and leave it close! Close it and let God present to you new opportunities so you can flourish in the things of God. Slam the Door! Take if off its hinges, Just don't go back in! When we tread areas of our life that God has told us to walk away from we are being disobedient to the calling he has stationed over our life.

I reflect on the story of Lots wife. She was told not to look back and out of disobedience she looked back and was turned into a pillar of salt. She was probably thinking like many of us today. She could do what she wanted to do and carry on through life like disobedience was a thing of the past.

There are many doors we must close because they lead into a path of ruin and defeat. There will be many doors that look like opportunities but in actuality they are pits filled with sin and death. I remember when God told me to close a door on a relationship with a guy I really loved; I kept trying to keep the door opened. As a result I endured a lot of heartache and pain. I went through a trouble season of depression, hurt, agony, and frustration. I couldn't understand why we couldn't get over the hurdles of our relationship. I now know that God was closing that door to prepare me for something and someone greater. Doors are like seasons they come and they go. We cannot force winter to stay in summer, and fall to stay in spring. Once the purpose is up it can never be fulfilled appropriately with a substitute.

Trying to keep a door open that is supposed to be closed is injurious to your spiritual well-being. This mindless effort will deplete you of the energy needed to walk in your ordained purpose. The other side of a closed door is opportunities, blessings, new beginnings, hope, love, joy, possibilities and dreams that are waiting for you to experience. In baseball the players get three strikes and their out, in life you aren't guaranteed anything so make sure you are walking through and closing the right doors.

I think I just heard a door slamming. I pray it was you closing the door to those things that may

overcome you.

What's standing On the Other Side of Your Door?

Slaying The Inner Giant

What is standing on the other side of your door?

Why do you need to close it?

What are some of barriers that are hindering you from closing it all the way?

Why are you afraid of closing this door?

Proverbs 24:14

Know that wisdom is such to your soul; if you find it, there will be a

future, and your hope will not be cut off.

LIVING LIFE STRAIGHT WITH NO CHASER

The 30 DAY CHALLENGE

SLAYING THE GIANT WITHIN

Day 16

Challenge: Divorce Your Infirmities

We all know David was a much smaller boy than Goliath. The odds of him killing Goliath was slim. David I know in the natural he was fearful. He looked at his 4 foot stature and then how much taller Goliath was over him. He may have looked at how strong Goliath was and he knew he only had the strength as a boy. However, David had to divorce his fear from his faith that day. He had to divorce the insecurities he had about not winning. David had to divorce his earthly strength and rely on the only weapon he had. He had to put down his secret fears and grab a hold of his slingshot.

The word for today is Divorce. I am not just speaking about the legal separation between husband and wife but the process of letting something go, letting things go, letting habits go, letting thought patterns go, letting negativity go, letting lifestyles go, letting methods and ideology go , letting go, period, point blank.

What are some things you need to divorce today? Prophetically I hear God saying, Cut the cord and live freely. He has confirmed that you will be able to breathe on your own after this, just let go! I know it is not easy to just go cold turkey and let go but sometimes it can be a life and death situation. Distress is very common in the process of letting go. Psalm 120:1 lets us know that in our distress we can cry unto the Lord and he will hear us. This scripture to me brings some comfort, but when you are going through the severing process it doesn't feel good. When a surgeon is preparing a patient for surgery, he doesn't tell them that the recovery process will be pain free. He doesn't guarantee them that they are going to be able to just get up off the operating table free from soreness and pain. When we are transitioning from a splitting or emotional separation we must know it's going to be a rigorous process attached to unease and restlessness.

I have had to experience two legal divorces in my life and one was very traumatic because it involved releasing my best friend, the father of my children, my prayer partner and someone who I loved dearly. I was letting go of a person that had been in my life since I was 13 years old. The releasing of this person was painful, although I knew that it was what we both had agreed upon it did not take away the anxieties and pain associated with it. I had to lean on Samuel 22:7. The word says, in my distress I called upon the Lord, and cried to my God: and he did hear my voice out of his temple, and my cry did enter his ears.

When we have to depart from someone, or something most times it will not be a day in the park, or an easy process, we will not feel good emotionally. The joy of letting go is knowing that God has a plan and he will surely deliver you from the dark to the light.

As we experience life we will be adjacent with many things that are unhealthy for us. We will become attached to people, places, things, habits, rituals, traditions, and lifestyle mannerisms that unfortunately will not be healthy for us. Letting go of things that we have become relaxed with is difficult. The reason these things become difficult is that we become too comfortable with certain things. Moving out of our comfort zone brings some spiritual soreness. With soreness it brings uneasiness, and uneasiness constitutes, irritability and irritability can evoke stress.

As men and women of God we must realize that while division, separation, severance and disconnection is excruciating it is sometimes needed to allow the healing process to take place. Everything we experience in life has a lesson attached to it.

Divorcing your Infirmities – Slaying The Inner Giant

Why is it so hard to let things that are unhealthy go out of our life?

What is the hardest thing you have had to release from your life?

What are some personal emotions associated with letting go?

Share an experience that you let go that has helped somebody else?

Psalm 136:1

Give thanks to the Lord because he is good. His love continues

forever.

LIVING LIFE STRAIGHT WITH NO CHASER

The 30 DAY CHALLENGE

SLAYING THE GIANT WITHIN

Day 17

Challenge: Appreciate his Goodness

When David killed Goliath he had an historical event to highlight. He could have just written it off as an everyday occurrence but, it was much more to him than just a playground brawl. It was an accomplishment .When God allows us to experience something where he gets the glory. We must highlight it.

The word for today is "Grab a Highlighter". There are many teachable moments that God has placed before you and you have failed to highlight it. There has been messages you have heard, life experiences along the way , conversations you been engaged in , things you have seen with your natural eyes, tragedies that have brought you to tears , triumphs that has been worth celebrating, new discoveries we have made, and nuggets of wisdom we have failed to highlight along our journey.

The purpose of highlighting something is for it to stand out and serve as a reminder that this information or event contains some substance that could be used in the future. I am excited when I read my Bible and see a passage of scripture that I had highlighted years or even months ago. Often the highlighted text jumps off the page like the "HOT LIGHT at Krispy Kreme doughnuts.

It begins to make my inner man leap because it knows that this word once served as a bridge over troubled waters.

We must not lose sight of opportunities to grab a highlighter and capture those moments of truth and revelation that God is presenting to us. In life we tend to take years, months, days, hours, minutes and seconds for granted. No man knows the day or the hour. So, therefore we must use each day as an opportunity to be appreciative of Gods goodness.

Have you ever thought that often the small things people say , ring true to our spirits (highlight it) Those pieces of wisdom that your grandmother said when you were 10 years old (highlight it) The comments your children make that surprise you (highlight it) The words your mate whisper in your ear (highlight it) The unexpected texts messages you receive during the day (highlight it) Keep a spiritual Highlighter in your heart at all times and highlight the moments that will help you through this journey called life.

We are given so many opportunities to have a teachable moment from God. You don't have to go to college for four long years to gain the wisdom and knowledge that God has positioned for you. Clinch the finer details of life. Hold on to the distinct particles of knowledge that you will need to be spiritually successful. Highlight the uniqueness of your day. Highlight the captivating thoughts that come across your mind. Capture the rewarding proficiencies that are given to you from God. I challenge you to grab your spiritual highlighter and begin to bask in the aroma of Jesus.

Highlight It- Slaying the Inner Giant

What are something's you would like to highlight?

What has God done for you this week that needs highlighting?

What has God done for your family or children that are worth highlighting?

What have you done that others may want to highlight?

Proverbs 24:14

Know that wisdom is such to your soul; if you find it, there will be a

future, and your hope will not be cut off.

LIVING LIFE STRAIGHT WITH NO CHASER

The 30 DAY CHALLENGE

Day 18

SLAYING THE GIANT WITHIN

Challenge: Revealing the Truth

WONT YOU JUST TELL THE TRUTH: Tell the truth had it not been for Jesus you would've been dead sleeping in your grave but God made old death behave. Tell the truth, you would've lost your mind when your baby daddy left you for another woman. Tell the truth , you could've been locked up in jail for stealing things you didn't even need but you didn't get caught isn't God a keeper.

Tell the truth, you could've been charged with D.W.I. all the times you drove home drunk or high from the clubs but God took over the wheel and allowed you to get home safely. Tell the truth, you could've had HIV or AIDS all the men and women you slept with unprotected but God protected your immune system. Tell the truth , you could've gone to jail for writing bad checks for forging other people checks but God supplied your financial needs right in the nick of time. Tell the truth, you could've gotten exposed for sleeping with that woman's/man husband or wife but God dissolved the relationship. Tell the truth, you could've lost your job for lying about being sick and not showing up but God gave you another chance. Tell the truth, you could've been exposed for all the lies you told, but God worked it out. Tell the truth, you could've lost your mind from all the demonic attacks that suffocated your mind over no deceptive men but God gave you a renewed mind. Tell the truth you could've been evicted from your home for spending the rent money trying to keep up with the Joneses but God keep shelter over your head, Tell the truth , you could've been addicted to crack, cocaine and weed but God snatched that high right out your mouth . Tell the truth, don't be ashamed of your testimony --- Tell It!

What does this scripture say to you?

Slaying The Inner Giant

"A truthful witness saves lives, but a false witness is a traitor"

Proverbs 14:25

Response:

Philippians 4:8

Brother and sisters, think about things that are good and worthy of

praise. Think about the things that are pure and honorable and

right and pure and beautiful and respected

LIVING LIFE STRAIGHT WITH NO CHASER

The 30 DAY CHALLENGE

Day 19

SLAYING THE GIANT WITHIN

Challenge: Unpack Your Baggage and Think on the Right Things

When I ask the question what is in your bag, I am not referring to the paper, plastic or even canvass bag. I am talking about your Spiritual, Emotional and Psychological bag. We all carry around baggage, rather it be a small change purse, a duffle bag or a large suitcase. We all have it. Some of us have designer baggage we just dress it up and carry it on our life shoulders trying to convince the world that we are expensive and okay ,when the truth is we are tore up from the floor up. We have issues that require tissues; we are just dressed up dirt.

Some of us carry around a Plastic bag and want to just recycle the hurt and pain. There are some that carry around the paper bag because we think it is more global and society will accept that. But, Lord some of us carry around that dingy duffle bag that has all our baggage and other people baggage. In the duffle bag we carry the baggage from our childhood, our last three relationships, our children's baggage, work baggage and our mama and daddy baggage.

Last but not least, there is that old out dated bag that consist of outdated mess and stress that we should've been thrown out years, months and weeks ago. Why do we hold on to BAGGAGE?, because we are comfortable with our mess, we don't value ourselves enough to throw that OLD mess away, We rather wallow in the pigs pen than to feast at the Masters table. We rather have a pity party instead of a Celebration of life; we rather live in the land of lack than Abundance Ave. We rather walk in weariness instead of walking it out with Jesus. We rather be the dumping ground for others than be a light in darkness. We rather talk about what we could've, would've or should've done instead of getting up and being proactive in our situations.

Decide today, right now that you NO longer work for Waste Management and get rid of all that waste and garbage out of your life. You deserve it; you are worthy to be set free from the garbage.

Are you ready to take out your trash? What sin is in your bag?

Slaying The Inner Giant

1.

2.

3.

4.

5.

6.

7.

8.

9.

10.

2 Corinthians 5:18

All this is from God, who through Christ reconciled us to himself

and gave us the ministry of reconciliation.

LIVING LIFE STRAIGHT WITH NO CHASER

The 30 DAY CHALLENGE

Day 20

SLAYING THE GIANT WITHIN

Challenge: Starting Over

After my divorce in 1999 I thought my world had come to an end. I couldn't fathom the thought that I was going to be a single mother of two school age children. At the time my children were 9 and 5. The process was a very frenzied process. I had to come to grips with the fact that I was no longer considered a married woman. I would now be classified as a single parent. The thought of being a single mother was very depressing and caused me a lot of anxieties. I was devastated for several reasons. One I was losing my best friend and two I felt I had let my children down.

Starting over to me meant failure. It meant I had failed at the most important assignment I had been given. To me it meant that my American dream was all a lie. All I could see was failure written in red across the sky every time I tried to look up.

What starting over taught me was that there is a light at the end of the tunnel .There was hope after the havoc. There was peace after the pain. There was joy after the Juggling of emotions. Even when we have to start over just know that God is with you. Through the process of starting over, we have to look for the lesson God is trying to teach us.

Today we will explore starting over. Sometimes we have to go back to the starting line and just START OVER. I thank God we have the opportunity to start over and correct some of the wrongs that we endured in our life.

While starting over we have to realize that we have the ability to experience forgiveness from our Father. Forgiveness is an essential process we must go through when starting over. It is a blessing to be able to have the option to repent and move forward even when everything around you looks so bleak. I had to start over many times in my life and I thank God for being a God of a 2nd 3rd and 4th chance.

My brothers and sisters never be to prideful to admit you failed. I encourage you to START OVER today! When starting over put fear, pride, doubt, procrastination, and seek God for guidance.

2 Corinthians 5:17 reminds us that when we start over we are being made into a new creature. Therefore if any man be in Christ, he is a new creature: **old things are passed away**; behold all things will become new.

Starting Over Quotes to Move Forward With: Slaying The Inner Giant

The greatest glory in living lies in never falling, but in rising every time we fall.

- Nelson Mandela

Success consists of going from failure to failure without loss of enthusiasm.

- Winston Churchill

The secret of getting started is breaking your complex overwhelming tasks

into small manageable tasks, and then starting on the first one.

- Mark Twain

The starting point of all achievement is desire.

- Napoleon Hill

Which one of these quotes best reflect the process of starting over for you and why?

LIVING LIFE STRAIGHT WITH NO CHASER

The 30 DAY CHALLENGE

SLAYING THE GIANT WITHIN

Day 21

Challenge: Embrace Truth

We all know the story of the boy who cried wolf. There once was a shepherd boy who was bored as he sat on the hillside watching the village sheep. To amuse himself he took a great breath and sang out, "Wolf! Wolf! The Wolf is chasing the sheep!" The villagers came running up the hill to help the boy drive the wolf away. But when they arrived at the top of the hill, they found no wolf. The boy laughed at the sight of their angry faces. "Don't cry 'wolf', shepherd boy," said the villagers, "When there's no wolf!" They went grumbling back down the hill. Later, the boy sang out again, "Wolf! Wolf! The wolf is chasing the sheep!" To his naughty delight, he watched the villagers run up the hill to help him drive the wolf away. When the villagers saw no wolf they sternly said, "Save your frightened song for when there is really something wrong! Don't cry 'wolf' when there is NO wolf!" But the boy just grinned and watched them go grumbling down the hill once more. Later, he saw a REAL wolf prowling about his flock. Alarmed, he leaped to his feet and sang out as loudly as he could, "Wolf! Wolf!" But the villagers thought he was trying to fool them again, and so they didn't come.

At sunset, everyone wondered why the shepherd boy hadn't returned to the village with their sheep. They went up the hill to find the boy. They found him weeping. There really was a wolf here! The flock has scattered! I cried out, "Wolf!" Why didn't you come?" An old man tried to comfort the boy as they walked back to the village. We'll help you look for the lost sheep in the morning," he said, putting his arm around the youth, the moral of the story is "Nobody believes a liar...even when he is telling the truth!"

Our life parallels this story many times. We lie to cover the truth. We convince ourselves that if we can just pretend that something is not what it is it will go away. Today I will help you expose the truth .Psalms 31:18, "Let the lying lips be put to silence. Living a life of lies only obstructs you from the blessings that God had intended for you to live. God is the only one that can give us a way of escape. Lying to ourselves and others is not a way to overcome but a way to stay defeated in our life. Chose to be victorious over the spirit of lying.

Truth Tidbits: - Slaying The Inner Giant

Psalm 119:160 the sum of your word is truth and every one of your righteous rules endures forever.

John 17:17 Sanctify them in the truth; your word is truth.

Job 34:12 of a truth, God will not do wickedly, and the Almighty will not pervert justice.

Psalm 25:5 Lead me in your truth and teach me, for you are the God of my salvation; for you I wait all the day long.

Which scripture deals with the spirit of lying and why?

Psalm 147:3

He healeth the broken in heart, and bindeth up their wounds

LIVING LIFE STRAIGHT WITH NO CHASER

The 30 DAY CHALLENGE

Day 22

SLAYING THE GIANT WITHIN

Challenge: Being Complete

What does it mean to be complete?

Whole: Having every necessary part or everything that is wanted, finished: having reached the normal or expected end, and absolute: being the greatest degree of something. After reviewing this definition, I realized that there were many things I had substituted in my life to feel complete. My list wasn't small it was large and deadly While on my search for wholeness I learned a lot about myself. The greatest unearthing is knowing one's self and accepting that you are not perfect and can use some improvements to capture your defined wholeness.

The word for today is COMPLETENESS. What completes you? As a woman I have been in a place where I thought a man completed me, only to find out that he was just dressed up, smelling good, dust, flesh and blood. He could NOT complete me .He is subject to fail me at any time. I have also resorted to food to fill that void and all I had left was a few extra pounds and a bad body image. I then tried to overcompensate with shopping (which I really dislike) only to realize that clothes didn't make me feel good either.

God is really all we need. When people come into our life they serve as a complimentary gift to accent the things we have already. We should love God and ourselves enough to be alright if people decide to walk away. However, the devil tricks us into depression and tells us we are not good enough, or that we are to imperfect to be accepted. All of that is a lie from the pits of hell.

When we are broken , fragmented or disjointed and feel incomplete in any area of our life we have to know that God is still in the mending, healing, and re-upholstery business (he was a carpenter remember) He can make us whole again. Some of the lessons we go through is just a testimony of our faith.

I have had some days when I felt worthless, hopeless and just downright speechless at the way things were going in my life, but God showed up right on time with spiritual nurses to mend my wounded heart and mind. To repair my brokenness, He picked up my shattered remnants, scraps and prickly particles and transformed me into the woman he knows he had designed me to be. If he did it for me, he can do it for you too. My daddy is not a respecter of persons. Do you want to be made whole? Well just tell your daddy about it. Repeat after me : I AM WHOLE , I AM WHOLE , I AM WHOLE ......

The woman with the issues of blood was incomplete. She had been living with an infirmity for 12 years and she felt incomplete. I can imagine she felt physically and emotionally sick. It wasn't until she touched the hem of his garment that she was made whole. Sometimes all it takes is a hem encounter.

Whatever issue is going on with you just know that wholeness and completeness comes from

God.

Wholeness Affirmations- Slaying The Inner Giant

Today I declare and decree, that I am complete. I speak to the brokenness in my life which is now made whole. I speak complete authority over all my fragmented pieces. I declare and decree that I will take responsibility for my life and all the things that held me in bondage. I will not allow anything or anybody to move me out of my place of freedom in Jesus Name Amen.

I am whole and I am free. There is nothing that can entrap me. I have made a choice to be free and free indeed. No more brokenness in my life.

I am stretching forth my hand to touch the hem of Jesus Garment. My goal is to be made whole. I am on a mission to be made whole in Jesus name.

I am no longer shattered glass. When I look in my mirror of miracles I am made whole. God has completed me.

Philippians 4:13

I can do all things though him who strengthens me.

LIVING LIFE STRAIGHT WITH NO CHASER

The 30 DAY CHALLENGE

Day 23

SLAYING THE GIANT WITHI

Challenge: Maintain Positivity

The word for today is Think Positive .When we are being pushed through a wilderness experience there is many rough and dry sceneries that we may encounter. During the wilderness experience nothing within our sight projects any life. Nothing seems positive. Everything around us seems flat and lifeless. Since things are so bland, it seems as though we can't hear the birds chirping, the sun doesn't seem to shine, the wind doesn't seem to blow, the earth doesn't seem to rotate on its axis, nothing seems right. The wilderness experience is one that leaves you feeling desolate and dry but really I believe God is teaching you to focus and concentrate on him and him only.

While in search of positivity, He is trying to remove all the hustle and bustle out of your life to prepare you for something greater. While in the wilderness you start to feel negative, and irritated. Everything within your grasp is unconstructive and it drowns your sense of hope and life. When in search of positivity, it seems like you will never find your way mentally through the brush and thickness of the forest. The wilderness experience prompts God to send you a personal Forest Ranger to help you find the right path that leads back to positivity.

While wondering through the negativity trail it seems like you are going to just die from the fatigue and weariness of going in circles. Thinking positively activates your spirit .Well today I want you to declare and decree that you have found your way out of negativity. You have found your way out of wilderness thoughts and actions. You have found your way out of wilderness drama. Speak positively over your life, Say: I am Healthy, Wealthy and WISE, I am the HEAD and NOT the Tail, I am an over comer, I shall LIVE and NOT DIE, I have a wonderful gift to give to the world. I am ALL that God says I am and more. I am Victorious over my situation. My mind will stay focused on the Lord, for he is the sustainer of my soul. I will be renewed in my mind, body and soul saith the Lord.

Meditate on the fact that everything that is positive comes from the Lord, and everything that is negative is generated from a negative source. Joshua 1:8 says keep this book of the law always on your lips; meditate on it day and night, so that you may be careful to do everything written in it. Then you will be prosperous and successful.

Positive Pin Points – Slaying The Inner Giant

1. What kind of positive things do you do to make it throughout the day, week, and month?

2. Do you surround yourself with positive people or negative people?

3. What affirmations do you read or repeat throughout the day to remain positive?

John 8:12

❖

Then spake Jesus unto them saying, I am the light of the world: he

that followeth me shall not walk in darkness, but shall have the light

of life.

LIVING LIFE STRAIGHT WITH NO CHASER

The 30 DAY CHALLENGE

Day 24

SLAYING THE GIANT WITHIN

Challenge: Maintaining Your Light

The word for today is GLOWIN THE OVERFLOW OF JESUS. Sometimes we get so entangled

with the cares of this world that we forget to let our light shine. We tend to dim our lights when

we are going through hard times ourselves. It is during those times that we should just shine

through even more. We have to realize that when God chose us to be lanterns unto the world he

is depending on us to shine through during the good and bad times. Just this week I was going

through a very emotional time. I felt low and downtrodden. At 3 am in the morning I had a friend

to call and ask for prayer for the same thing I was going through. I could have chosen to blow

my light completely out and not answer but God recharged the batteries in my flashlight and

allowed me to minister to her in her time of darkness. God will meet you right where you are. It

is during the storm that we must not put away our spiritual umbrella. It is during these times we

must put on the whole amour of God and allow him to manifest a victory through us. It is so

amazing to me that God told us in Isaiah 2:5 that we are to walk in the light of the Lord. To me

this passage of scripture is saying that while we may walk in darkness; just know that God is with us as the light. We are not to be distracted by dark episodes in our life. We are to execute the light that resides in the inside of us and walk according to the word of God.

As Christians sometimes our light is the only light that many sinners will see on their journey and if we continue to let our light be dimmed it will not be a good witness before others. Light symbolizes truth. Light reveals the things that are hidden within the consciousness of our hearts and minds. Light is the absence of darkness. Light symbolizes God's salvation for mankind. Matthew 5:16 says. In the same way, let your light shine before men, that they may see your good deeds and praise your Father in Heaven.

We have to GLOW IN THE OVERFLOW OF JESUS. As men and women of God we have to continue to let our light shine because there has already been somebody assigned to you for a word of encouragement or an act of kindness. God has already equipped us with everything we need to GLOW. He has given us a testimony, the word, love, peace, empathy, compassion, faith, courage, and so much more to keep shining through this dim and grim world in which we live. GLOW IN THE OVERFLOW.

I know every day will not be a bright day but let that little light of yours shine. Let it shine in your home, job, community, and church. Whatever your wattage is, let it shine. GLOW IN THE OVERFLOW OF JESUS! No matter how dark it gets in your cave, keep looking up and there will be light shining through soon. Jesus is the true light of the world and that makes us flickers of light because we are his ... GLOW IN THE OVERFLOW OF JESUS. Sisters and Brothers when we walk into room things should get brighter. When we walk into a problem it is our light

that navigates us through. Why because we are GLOWING IN THE OVERFLOW OF JESUS

Will you let your light shine today? Go ahead I dare you to shine.

Maintaining Your Light – Slaying The Inner Giant

What are some ways you are allowing your light to shine?

A)

B)

C)

D)

E)

F)

Colossians 3:16

❖

Let the word of Christ richly dwell within you, with all wisdom

teaching and admonishing one another with psalms and hymns and

spiritual song with thanksgiving in your hearts to God.

LIVING LIFE STRAIGHT WITH NO CHASER

The 30 DAY CHALLENGE

Day 25

SLAYING THE GIANT WITHIN

Challenge: Having the Right Conversation

The word for today is having the right conversation. Some of us are involved in all types of chat

groups, phone links, texting dialogues and etc., but many of us are not having the right

conversations. We spend more time talking about nothing. We need to learn to have the right

conversation.

Instead of us calling our Pastor, friends and family every time a storm arises we need to be

tucking ourselves away and having a conversation with our Savior Jesus Christ. Our father is

only a word away, a breath away, a thought away. For he knows what we are thinking and going

through before we even mutter one word. All we have to do is call out his name and start to talk.

God likes to hear our praises but a general conversation with him is what he can best relate to. Be

real with God tell him what hurts and what you feel. Tell him how you messed up, how you took

a wrong turn. He knows all these things anyway. An intimate conversation with God is

unexplainable. It is like an orgasm to the soul. (Yes, I said it) It helps us to release those extra

tensions.

Have the right conversation (Testimony) My daddy has been waking me up at 4am the last 5 days and I just get up and talk to him and pour out my heart to him. I tell him how I feel about all the hurt and pain. I share my fears and concerns. I pray for those I feel have offended me. I just pour it all out and he just loves on me and listens. After I talk, I then listen and he speaks to my spirit. I feel so refreshed afterwards. We have to learn to push aside worldly conversations that don't lead to salvation, love, solutions, edification, or peace. Nonsense talking is mindless jibber-jabber. When people call you and the conversation hold no substance be bold enough to end it. I am talking about gossip. We have to do away with vain words being deposited into our spirit. Having the right conversation is what counts. Having the right conversation is what will reveal the true substance of your spiritual character.

Have you ever had a friend that calls you and they are always just full of conversation that have no substance but when you begin to talk about the goodness of God they seem twitchy and annoyed? Well it is probably a good time to address the issue of how you will not tolerate gossip in your life and entertain conversations that contain no core elements that will help lift up the kingdom.

The one conversation that appeals to me is the conversation that Jesus had with his disciples during the last supper. Jesus had to farewell his disciples. John 14:1 He shared with them, "Do not let your heart be troubled, Trust in God, trust also in me. The conversation could have gone in another direction but he wanted to make sure that he was having the right type of conversation. The conversation was to comfort his disciples. When you are having a conversation with someone it should serve as a way to comfort and reassure. We shouldn't let our light go muted because we are being judgmental, bias, confrontational or hypercritical. When Jesus spoke to others he offered them hope and encouragement . He made sure he was having the right conversation. He made sure he was speaking life into others and not damnation, revenge or hate. Regardless of how Jesus was treated during the crucifixion. He never said a mumbling word. Even through this process he was asking his father to forgive those that had falsely accused him. He was having the right conversation. He was still encouraging others. I don't know if I could have shut up and allowed others to take my life so humbly. One of my stumbling blocks while on this journey was my mouth. My conversations weren't always Godly. Let's make sure we are having the right conversation so others can see God in us. There used to be a song that the older saints use to sing, it was Jesus is on the main line tell him what you want. The song was basically saying communicate with God. Well here's your opportunity. Start right now.

Communication with God, Having the Right Conversation –

Slaying The Inner Giant

If anyone speaks, he should do it as one speaking the very words of God. (1 Peter 4:11)

The tongue has the power of life and death.

(Proverbs 18:21)

Men will have to give account on the Day of Judgment for every careless word they have

spoken. (Matthew 12:36)

He who guards his lips guards his life, but he who speaks rashly will come to ruin. (Proverbs

13:3)

With the tongue we praise our Lord and Father, and with it we curse men, who have been made

in God's likeness. Out of the same mouth come praise and cursing. (James 3:9-10)

The mouth of the righteous is a fountain of life, but overwhelms the mouth of the wicked.

(Proverbs 10:11)

The lips of the righteous nourish many, but fools die for lack of judgment. (Proverbs 10:21)

I have resolved that my mouth will not sin. (Psalm 17:3)

From the fruit of his lips a man is filled with good things as surely as the work of his hands rewards him. (Proverbs 12:14)

From the fruit of his mouth a man's stomach is filled; with the harvest from his lips he is satisfied. (Proverbs 18:20)

The quiet words of the wise are more to be heeded than the shouts of a ruler of fools. (Ecclesiastes 9:17)

Through patience a ruler can be persuaded, and a gentle tongue can break a bone. (Proverbs 25:15)

The tongue of the wise commends knowledge, but the mouth of the fool gushes folly. (Proverbs 15:2)

No man can tame the tongue. It is a restless evil, full of deadly poison. (James 3:8)

Reckless words pierce like a sword, but the tongue of the wise brings healing. (Proverbs 12:18)

LIVING LIFE STRAIGHT WITH NO CHASER

The 30 DAY CHALLENGE

SLAYING THE GIANT WITHIN

Day 26

Challenge: Being True To Yourself

The word for today is " BE TRUE TO YOURSELF" I know there are things that we know about others that just make us cringe, but what about the things you know about yourself, how are you dealing with those things? We have to learn to be true to ourselves. I know there are things about Sabriena that I do not like and if anyone else knew about them I would be ashamed.

 The truth is there is nothing that we can hide from God. When we know there is areas in our dusty life that need healing and deliverance we should not push it under the rug. We have to identify our strengths and weaknesses and work on the things that keep us separated from God. BEING TRUE TO YOURSELF is acknowledging that you are an imperfect being and you are messed up and need an intervention from God.

The best interventionist is Jesus Christ. No matter what your hidden hangs up are, God is ready to help you. We have to expose our secret sins and rely on a savior who can save you. The enemy wants to keep us bound in our sinful nature. BE TRUE YOURSELF AND CRY OUT LORD HELP ME!

Bring all your filthy flaws to him and he will surely clean you up. Come on y'all we have to just be real and come from behind the veil. In an AA meeting they start out hello my name is _____ and I am an alcoholic. Well in your deliverance meeting say my name is _____ and I am a _____. Will you be TRUE TO YOURSELF today? GIVE IT TO ME STRAIGHT WITH NO CHASER. When we can accept the fact that we were made in God's image and he doesn't make any junk. We should be more confident in knowing whose we are in Christ. Being true to yourself involves first knowing who you are , acknowledging your strength and weaknesses, working on the areas that need attention , forgiving yourself from any past flaws and allowing God to heal you from the inside out . Being true to yourself is not allowing the criticism and doubt of others to invade your life and cause you to self-doubt yourself. Being true to yourself is walking in the purpose God has set before you. Being true to yourself is defining your destiny. Being true to yourself is allowing God to mold and shape you into the person that he knew when he conceived you in your mother's womb. We must never try to be anyone else other than ourselves because the purpose on the inside of us is connected to the kingdom and the full plan God has for us. I recommend you start to love you. Be true to you. When you fall short and start to lose hope in yourself, ask God to help you and he will come and help you redefine yourself.

When you look in a mirror, who do you see? Do you believe that the person you see can accomplish all things through Christ? Do you feel you were created with a purpose? Do you love yourself? Are you willing to work through your flaws? Are you worth loving yourself? Ponder

on this questions and work towards loving yourself and then work towards loving others.

Quotes about Loving One's Self

"Why are you trying so hard to fit in when you were born to stand out?"
Ian Wallace

"Love yourself. Forgive yourself. Be true to yourself. How you treat yourself sets the standard for how others will treat you."
Steve Marroboli

"

"BELIEVE in yourself even if nobody else does!"
Stephanie Lahart

"Encourage yourself, believe in yourself, and love yourself. Never doubt who you are."
Stephanie Lahart

"He leans over and takes her hand. With the other he touches her face. 'You your best thing, Sethe. You are.' His holding fingers are holding hers.

'Me? Me?"
Toni Morrison

"We must be our own authentically unique truth, and question who we are, what created us, and what processes within us are alien and externally created."
Bryant McGill

"We must step out of our digital avatars, and come together and have face-to-face dialogue as often as possible."

Bryant McGill

Psalm 55: 14

We had a good friendship and walked together to God's Temple.

LIVING LIFE STRAIGHT WITH NO CHASER

The 30 DAY CHALLENGE

Day 27

SLAYING THE GIANT WITHIN

Challenge: Building Healthy Relationships

The word for today is Relationship. What types of relationships are you developing, cultivating, and linked to at this point in your life? Is the relationship(s) you're in HEALTHY or UNHEALTHY?

In our lifetime many of us will encounter an unhealthy relationship, which may bring on many emotions, feelings, and perceptions of others that can eventually hinder future relationships we may encounter.

I can give an account of an intimate partner relationship that I was in that was very emotionally unhealthy. I tried to hold on to the person because I was afraid of being alone. I tried to do everything within my power to prove to this person that I loved them, when ultimately while pursuing this relationship, I was not loving myself. I realized that I was depositing all the love into a person who was unwilling to deposit anything healthy into me. I eventually had to investigate why I allowed people to walk all over me emotionally. The reason stemmed from the fact that I have always had a problem with abandonment.

I realized that in life People will withdraw from your life and leave you high and dry, and when it is time for us to withdraw from them they have insufficient time, energy, love, feelings, commitment or desire to maintain a relationship with you. Deuteronomy 31:8 says it is the Lord who goes before you. He will be with you; he will not leave you or forsake you. Do not fear or be dismayed. Unhealthy relationships can serve as hindrance in going forth in the things of God. Ask God to show you, who is for you and who is against you. Not everyone is going to be for you. Not everyone was for Jesus either. Judas had walked with Jesus. Jesus knew the relationship was unhealthy and Judas would betray him. Ask God who should be with you while you are pursuing Kingdom things.

Healthy or Unhealthy Choices – Slaying The Inner Giant

Please give an account when you made healthy or unhealthy choices. Please write down scenarios you have experienced either healthy or unhealthy. Share how you have matured or stayed the same.

Intimate Partner Relationship –

Friendship –

Work Relationship –

Family Relationship-

Deuteronomy 31:6

Be strong and courageous. Do not fear or be in dread of them, for it is the Lord your God who goes with you. He will not leave you or forsake you."

LIVING LIFE STRAIGHT WITH NO CHASER

The 30 DAY CHALLENGE

SLAYING THE GIANT WITHIN

Day 28

Challenge: Strengthening Your Heart

Our heart is the strongest organ in our body. Our heart is the one organ that we cannot live

without and properly function as a human being. Our heart is one big muscle that works really

hard to keep our other organs functioning. If the heart is this super organ then why is it always

broken emotionally? Why when someone has a rough ending to a relationship they describe it as

having their heart broken? Can broken hearts be mended? Is this something a modern day

surgeon can repair or is it Gods job to make all hurt be healed.

The word for today is "YOU CAN REBOUND AFTER A HEART INVASION?" The answer

to that question is yes; you can rebound, recover, bounce back, and survive a heart invasion.

Jesus Christ our redeemer is a great heart fixer and mind regulator. So what if someone came

along and invaded your mind with lies, deceit and pain. We have to remember there is absolutely

nothing to hard for God. God likes to take your tears and turn them into triumph. He likes to take

our brokenness and multiply it with blessings. He longs to prosper you through your pain, and heal you through all the heartache. We sometimes don't see the attack coming but God does and he is preparing us for the ATTACK even when we are unaware.

We sometimes leave our heart doors open and the ATTACKER doesn't have to literally knock down our door to get in, he just walks right in and before we know it he/ she is in our heart invading our self-esteem, self-worth, pride, possessions, goals, dreams, desire, image, finances and etc. I was once in a relationship where the guy wasn't working a steady job and I had more income. He was a real smooth talker and before I know it I was paying for dinners and treating him to lavish vacations. He would always make promises but none of them was being fulfilled. He had snuck right up on me and before I knew what was happening, my heart had been invaded and so was my credit and income.

Proverbs 4:23 tells us above all else, guard your heart, for everything you do flows from it. Philippians 4:6-7 reminds us that our heart is not the blood pump in your chest, but it is the core of your being; your spirit man lives within. Matthew 22: 37 encourage us to love the Lord your God with all your heart and with all your soul and with your entire mind. Jeremiah 17:9-10 says the heart is deceitful above all things, and desperately wicked: who can know it? My answer to that is God. God is the only one who can know our heart intentions and heal it when it is broken. 1 Samuel 16:7 gives us comfort in this scripture when he says to Samuel " Do not look in his appearance or on the height of his stature, because I have rejected him; for the Lord sees not as man sees; man looks on the outward appearance , but the Lord looks on the heart. Luke 6:45

says a good man produces good deeds from his hidden wickedness. Whatever is in the heart overflows into speech?

In order to deter a heart invasion one must, build a security system around your heart: Build it with prayer, intercession, and positive fellowship, knowing the word and a right relationship with God. Set the alarm to go off when an intruder is lurking on the borders of your heart. Remember, you can rebound after a HEART INVASION!

Heart Invasion – Slaying The Inner Giant

Write your testimony on how God rescued you from a Heart Invasion. How did you survive? What advice could you share with others?

John 14:23-24

Jesus answered him, "If anyone loves me, he will keep my word, and my Father will love him, and we will come to him and make our home with him. Whoever does not love me does not keep my words. And the word that you heart is not mine but the Fathers who sent me.

LIVING LIFE STRAIGHT WITH NO CHASER

The 30 DAY CHALLENGE

Day 29

SLAYING THE GIANT WITHIN

Challenge: Check Yourself, What's your Worth?

When we are doing some shopping and have a limited budget, we pay close attention to what we are placing in the basket and our objective is not to over spend. If the cashier over charge us we are quick to check our receipt to see where we have been overcharged. If we are overcharged we march over to customer service to get a refund.

How come we don't double check our life receipt and see where the devil is overcharging us and putting us in spiritual debt. The devil has been placing things in our spiritual basket and because we haven't been paying attention, he has been charging a lot of negativity, stress, and mess in our life. God is sending us a warning that we must check our life receipt and find out what we are worth. There is a cost in being a woman and man of God. We can't have a life of cheap character and inexpensive integrity. You have to live a life of knowing your worth. You are a daughter or son of the most high God and he desires that you live a life that represents that. You can't live a life as a child of God feeling unworthy, and not knowing your spiritual worth. You have to know whose you are in Christ. You must evaluate your life and know where you stand in

Christ. When the enemy comes at you, you should have enough confidence to stand up against him and let him know whose you are in Christ.

The word for today is Check Your Receipt. We need to check our life receipt and see if we are purchasing/ pursuing the right items for our life or are we just grabbing things, people and principles because they are cheap and we want the cheap way out? Are we purchasing/ pursuing the good quality items that will last and add substance to our life? Are we chasing after things because they are on-sale such as the latest fads? In life we have to learn to check ourselves. What are we idolizing, what are we searching after? What message are we trying to send to the world? There was a craze a few years back where people left the tags on their clothes to show the value of it. Well is that all we are worth the monetary value of stuff? CHECK YOUR RECEIPT.... ON YOUR RECEIPT YOU SHOULD FIND: some fruit-fruits of the Spirit, Meat- The word of God, vegetables-good substance and nutrients, bread- holy manna, wine- The blood of Jesus and other spiritual tools that will enhance the kingdom of God. CHECK YOUR RECEIPT, IF YOU DONT FIND ANY OF THESE THINGS THERE, empty out your basket and ask God for a refund. When shopping through life remember a deal is not always a deal unless you grab a hold of the FREE OFFER and that is SALVATION. Are you going to check your receipt?

Check Your Receipt Evaluation

Who are you in Christ?

What Christian qualities do you possess?

What are some things you need to return to the world because it is becoming a distraction?

What areas of your life are you allowing others to get free items that should be attached to a kingdom price?

How do you feel about yourself?

Mind

Body

Soul

If you had to rate yourself Spiritually, How would you rate yourself on a scale of 1-10 and why?

Score ___ 1 – Lowest, 10 Highest

Why:

Philippians 3:14

I press on towards the goal for the prize of the upward call of God in

Christ Jesus

LIVING LIFE STRAIGHT WITH NO CHASER

The 30 DAY CHALLENGE

Day 30

SLAYING THE GIANT WITHIN

Challenge: Don't Stop Pressing

What does it mean to press? Press means to move or cause to move into a position of contact with something by exerting continuous physical force. Press is to act upon through steady pushing or thrusting force exerted in contact. To try hard to persuade, to move by means of pressure. To insist on or request urgently. Well what does it mean to press in the spirit? Hosea 6:3 says: Let us acknowledge the Lord; let us press on to acknowledge him. As surely as the sun rises, he will appear, he will come to us like the winter rains, like the spring rains that water the earth.

The word for today is PRESS. You know how we use to press those jeans and put a crease in them because we don't want a wrinkle in them. Well we have to use as much pressure and force and PRESS those things in our life that holds us in a wrinkled status. PRESS those bad habits out, PRESS those ugly things we harbor in our hearts, PRESS those nasty feelings we have for one another, PRESS those things that hold us captive in fear. PRESS those things from our past that hold us hostage .Press OUT those insecurities and self-doubt We have to really PRESS and move to the place that God has ordained for us . Get your STARCH out - It is the word of God,

faith and Prayer! PRESS those Wrinkles out and Give God some glory ～～～ Amen

You have made it to day 30. You have challenged yourself to PRESS through the other 29 days

and challenge the inner giant that resides on the inside.

LIVING LIFE STRAIGHT WITH NO CHASER

The 30 DAY CHALLENGE

SLAYING THE GIANT WITHIN

Day: Bonus Day!

Challenge: How to Live Life God's Style

An individual has not started living until he can rise above the narrow confines of his

individualistic concerns to the broader concerns of all humanity.

Martin Luther King Jr.

Martin Luther King says it well "We must live and rise above the average standards set before

us."

 When I was growing up a young girl in the 70's , many adults us told me that I needed to reach

for the stars , but no one told me how far the stars were. No one explained there was an infinity

and beyond. No one shared with me what life consisted of, and all the pitfalls that I would face if

I made poor choices. No one shared with me that life has pitfalls and life came with heartaches

and disappoints.   All I was told is don't get pregnant before you are married and get a college

degree, and then you will have a happy life. Well I struggled to follow this advice and found that

it was not the solution to a happy life. After experiencing many life altering circumstances I

came to realize that loving myself, loving others and living for Christ was truly living. Many people do not get the message in this order so it led to a life of many failed experiences, unfulfilled dreams, and unmet goals. Today we will explore what it means to Live.

The word for today is LIVE. **L**- Learn to appreciate the simple things in life, so when your bountiful blessings manifest your will be prepared and equipped to receive it. **I**-Include LOVE in your life. Love people despite their past failures. Most importantly LOVE yourself. **V**- Live a Victorious life. Know that God already won the battle so VICTORY is already yours. **E**-Evaluate your purpose in life and LIVE life likes it's GOLDEN....... How are you living? GIVE IT TO ME STRAIGHT WITH NO CHASER~~~

There are several simple things in life that we unconsciously overlook. A smile, breath in your nostril, and love. A simple smile is evidence that you are living and there is joy present within. Waking up with fresh breath in your body is confirmation that God is with you and has a purpose for your life. Love shown and reciprocated is proof that you are in the family of Jesus Christ. Love is one of the greatest commandments. Mark 12:28-34 reminds us that we are to love the Lord your God with all your heart and with all your soul and with your entire mind and with all your strength. The second is this: 'Love your neighbor as yourself.' There is no commandment greater than these."

Apart of living life is living life victorious. So, one may ask how do you live life victorious? Well to live life victorious, one must live life to fulfill the purpose ordained for their life. Living life victorious is sharing and giving joy, peace, love, wisdom, forgiveness and exploring the fullness of God in everything you do. While living life victorious, life can be incomplete if we are not living life through purpose.

What is Purpose? According to the Bible, our purpose is the reason we are here, is for God's glory. In other words, our purpose is to praise God, worship him, to proclaim his greatness, and to accomplish his will. This is what glorifies him. Therefore, in this we find that God has given us a reason for our existence, a meaning for our existence. We were created by him, according to his desire, and our lives are to be lived for him so that we might accomplish what he has for us to do. When we trust the one who has made us, who works all things after the counsel of his will Ephesians 1:11, then we are able to live a life of purpose. How the particulars of that purpose are expressed is up to the individual.

Evaluate your purpose and be true to the assignment that God has given you. When we truly live our life true to our purpose we are pleasing unto God. I believe the only reason we were created was to carry out the purpose that God has deposited into us from our mother's womb. I will share my purpose. I knew from a little girl that God had created me to encourage others, and to love others unconditionally. My purpose was to speak life and hope into the life of others who may be weary on their journey through this place called life. My purpose is to help others walk into their ordained destiny and purpose. To allow others to operate in their gifts , through their own uniqueness. As a result of me walking in my purpose, I have been able to help others execute their dreams. I can honestly say, I am living my life with purpose.

What does this Quote say to you?

"I think the purpose of life is to be useful, to be responsible, to be honorable, and to be compassionate. It is, after all, to matter: to count, to stand for something, to have made some difference that you lived at all "– Leo C. Rosten

LIVING LIFE STRAIGHT WITH NO CHASER

Affirmation Day

Challenge: Celebrate

SLAYING THE GIANT WITHIN

The word for today is Celebration. You have made it to Day 30. This is a great start to Living Life Straight with No Chaser. There is cause to celebrate. There is a need to party; there is a requirement to have a festivity, and a reason for commemoration that you have boldly and successfully met the challenge that was set before you. You have addressed some very tough issues on this 30 day challenge and I pray that you have done a self- evaluation, and your spiritual weights are much lighter. After confronting some of your challenges I hope you are now able to bench press the stress and mess that has tried to enslave you on this journey called life.

During this 30 day challenge my prayer is that you have researched your mind, heart, body and soul. While re-examining yourself, I hope that you have decided to make some life altering changes that will eventually spark the light that is embedded on the inside of you. I hope that each challenge has given you the opportunity to think about your individual life and prayerfully you will be able to make some wrongs right and allow God to repair, restore and recapture the things that may have been ripped out of your life.

Reflect on each challenge and see how you can apply these principles into your life. Allow these challenge principles to become a way of life for you. Set aside your own wisdom and lean not unto your own understanding but totally trust in God to bring the healing, deliverance and direction that you need.

Living Life Straight with No Chaser – Slaying the Giant Within was written to give you the chance to address some issues in your life head on. It is a personal insight into your own life without judgment and criticism. It is an up close and personal mirror for you to gaze into and reflect on what you see in your personal life. I hope this 30 day challenge has allowed you to become a better person. I challenge you to continue to grow inwardly and love and live out loud. I now summon you to celebrate and live your life FREELY. You are now free to change your mindset, release the toxic baggage, refuse to accept negativity from others, close the door, face truths, become transparent , inhale –exhale, decide to live, release negativity, let go and let God, unlock your destiny, love unconditionally, submit , have expectations, know that closure is important, divorce your infirmities, appreciate the small things, reveal the truth , unpack your baggage, learn how to start over , embrace truth , be complete, maintain positivity, maintain your light , have the right conversation, be true to yourself check yourself, build healthy relationships , strengthen your heart, don't stop pressing and live life Gods style.

The challenge wasn't that bad was it? You survived and now you can walk into your destiny and

purpose with less pressure or weights that may try to weigh you down. After reading this book

please email me and share how these principles have affected your life. This 30 day challenge is

good to share in bible studies, discussion groups, family time, and so much more.

Visionary Sabriena Williams Bio:

Sabriena Williams developed the gift of creative writing at the early age of 12, when she inscribed her daily thoughts in a diary. Today her passion for writing has led to the publication of three books with five others awaiting debut. Sabriena is a native of Gainesville, FL. She received her A.A. Degree in general studies from Edwards Waters College in Jacksonville, FL, then proceeded to Bethune Cookman University, In Daytona Beach, FL where she obtained her B.S. degree in Psychology. She later pursued her M.S. in mental health counseling from Nova Southeastern University in Davie, FL.

Sabriena is the proud mother of two wonderful young adults: Ja'kyaRomea, 22, and Je'rod Harvey 19. She currently works as a Family Support Facilitator for a Non-Profit organization in Gainesville, Fl.

She is an astounding author of three power packed books: An Inspirational Touch: Embracing the Touch from God, which was released in 2006 - Christian Fiction "Wait on the Lord, I say Wait (spring 2010) and The Chocolate Drip published in (2012).

Sabriena is the Visionary of Total Vision Ministries an Outreach Ministry whose mission is to empower women into pursuing their purpose while strengthening their relationship with God. The ministry serves women from all denominations, race, age groups, and economic status. Total Vision was birthed in 2004. Apart of Total Vision ministries is the Woman at the Well Tour. The Woman at the WELL tour is an outreach ministry that offers healing and deliverance services for church women ministries and women groups. To date the W. A.T.W. tour has toured Florida and North Carolina. The W. A.T. W. Tour consist of seven women speaker all from different churches and denominations , praise dancers, A praise and worship leader, Gospel dramatization dept. and so much more. Total Vision Ministries also has a daily text message ministry, where the ministry has over 75 subscribers.

Sabriena was ordained as pastor in 2009 under the leadership of Bishop Sheldon McCray @ New Birth Sounds of Thunder Ministries in Greensboro, NC. She hopes to use her God given talents and gifts to spread the word of God through ministry, via outreach, book writings- signings, plays/productions, speaking engagements and personal interaction to help heal a wounded world one soul at a time.

Although Sabriena has been called a Pastor, Preacher, Teacher, Prophetess, Evangelist, and Spiritual Life Coach, however the one title she holds dear to her heart is Servant of God. Among her many accomplishments, In 2012 Sabriena was nominated for the Spirit of Gainesville award for her community involvement.

Contact Information

Email

Sabrienawilliams@gmail.com

Website:

www.totalvisionministry.com

Face Book:

Queenvision/Sabrienawilliams@FaceBook.com

Twitter: Passsionateabout@twitter.com

Phone Contact: 352-275-3549

CPSIA information can be obtained at www.ICGtesting.com
Printed in the USA
LVOW09s2237130114

369318LV00014B/219/P